Leading Ministry Time

Elijah Stephens

Leading Ministry Time
Copyright © 2015 by Elijah Stephens

ISBN: 069239401X
ISBN-13: 978-0692394014

Endorsements

Elijah Stephens has created a great tool for leading ministry time in this book. He uses fun, but helpful illustrations to describe what frequently happens in ministry times. He shares his own past successes and failures in such situations. He covers a variety of topics like: what's my role, how to facilitate ministry time, how to handle difficult situations, and how to overcome your own fears. He takes the process all the way from leading a small group to leading large groups through corporate ministry time. It is a great resource for those who want to see God move powerfully during the ministry times they lead.

Steve Backlund
Global Legacy Leader| Founder of Igniting Hope
GlobalLegacy.com | IgnitingHope.com

Some of us have been "lit up" by God's power but don't know how to grow in it, or lead others to minister in power. From his years of experience, Elijah has written a very practical, "how-to" guide enabling you to partner with the Holy Spirit as you teach a group of fellow believers to cooperate with Holy Spirit's ministry. With a pastor's heart to see people thrive and experience God's value for them, this book creates confidence that we can produce a community that ministers in power and mutual respect.

Dann Farrelly
Dean of Bethel's School of Supernatural Ministry
BSSM.net | iBethel.org

I've known Elijah Stephens since he was a wet-behind-the-ears college student. Ever since I've known him he has had a passion for teaching people how to partner with the Holy Spirit in bringing healing to people. In this book, Elijah outlines a clear guide to help ministry teams pray for people effectively. It will become a staple for training at our church.

Jeff Anderle
Senior Pastor
VineyardChattanooga.com

DEDICATION

To the love of my life, Alison. You are a ten.

Forward

Welcome to the new Reformation! Five hundred years ago Luther reasserted the concept of the priesthood of every believer but little was done to make that vision a reality. Ministry remained in the hands of the few and all others were relegated to the role of spectator. Thankfully, over the last few decades, there has been a growing awareness that every follower of Jesus is called to serve the Lord in both natural and supernatural ways, in every area of life. In order to fuel this new reformation, we need a wide variety of training materials that are biblical, accessible and practical, and this is why I love the book, *Leading Ministry Time*, by Elijah Stephens.

Elijah is a good friend and co-worker who has played a key role in the development of PastorsCoach.com. He is a true equipper who is passionate about helping people grow in knowledge, character, and ministry skills. Drawing from almost a decade as an executive pastor in a Vineyard church, Elijah draws insights from John Wimber, Bill Johnson, and other church leaders and combines them with his own practical experience to produce an excellent manual that can help train everyone from the senior pastor to the emerging small group leader.

Although Elijah teaches on many different aspects of ministry and church life, in this particular book he focuses almost exclusively on the topic of Ministry Time. For those who are unfamiliar with this term, it is the phrase most commonly used to describe the part of large group or small group gathering in which we take time to provide personal ministry for individuals and pray for specific needs. This can include prayer for healing, provision, direction or some form of deliverance. This kind of prayer and ministry requires a growing sensitivity to the Holy Spirit and an ever-increasing understanding of the supernatural realm. Elijah provides simple and effective training on hearing the voice of God, ministering in the prophetic and cooperating with the Spirit in various aspects of ministry.

In this book, Elijah helps the user to understand the potential power of "Ministry Time" but also the potential harm that can be done if this time is not led in a helpful and healthy manner. He provides excellent training on group dynamics and how to troubleshoot challenging situations and cope with difficult people. This book also teaches leaders how to cultivate and sustain an atmosphere and culture that will ensure the highest possible results with the least possible difficulties. This book is a must-read for anyone who aspires to minister effectively in the presence and power of God.

Michael Brodeur,
Founder of Pastor's Coach and Destiny Finder
PastorsCoach.com | DestinyFinder.com | MichaelBrodeur.com

CONTENTS

ACKNOWLEDGMENTS

I want to thank Caris Holliman, Anya Johnson, Leah Sookoo, and Dann Farrelly for helping edit and refine this content.

i

MINISTRY TIME

Ministry time is when believers intentionally set aside time to partner with Jesus to do supernatural ministry. It can happen anywhere: in a small group, after a service, in the streets, or in a bar.

Some of the most amazing experiences of my life have happened during ministry time. I've seen demons cast out of people; I've heard prophetic words so accurate that they made my hair stand on end; and I saw my wife healed from over 12 years of back pain.

Likewise, some of the saddest stories I have heard have happened during ministry time. A friend of mine shared with me that when he was in high school, he dated a girl who was terminally ill with cancer. They regularly got prayer from their church's prayer team, and yet after a long battle, she died. Later one of the team members approached him and said that she would still be alive if he had more faith. It hurt him deeply.

Once, at the end of a service, I went to the front of the sanctuary to get prayer. I stood in the altar area with my eyes closed to connect with God. While I was doing that, the speaker walked over to me and pushed me in the stomach as hard as he could in order to 'knock me out in the Spirit'. I flew forward, my face hitting his microphone. When I stood up, blood was gushing from my lip. I left the sanctuary asking myself, *How could someone do something like that in the name of Jesus?*

I share these stories so you can see that ministry time can be both helpful and harmful for the cause of Christ. Randy Clark puts it best when he said, "It's like nitroglycerin: if it is used the right way it is very powerful stuff. If it is used the wrong way, it is very powerful stuff." Ministry time is risky because for every potential benefit there is an equal and opposite danger. I've outlined some examples in the following chart so you can get a better idea of what these look like.

Benefits:	Dangers:
Healing People get healed emotionally, physically, and spiritually.	**Harm** People are damaged emotionally, physically, and spiritually.
Prophecy People receive clear and accurate words from the Lord. The words are properly judged.	**Manipulation** A personal agenda is presented as the word of God.
Deliverance People are set free from addictions, sin, and the demonic.	**Spiritual Abuse** Overzealous prayer ministers cross a person's boundaries in a way that dishonors the person and God.
Authentic Manifestations The Spirit touches people.	**Calling Attention to Ourselves** People fake manifestations in order to look spiritual.
Unity People are drawn closer to each other and Jesus as they see God move.	**Division** People are pushed further away from God and each other.

These facts should convince leaders to think deeply about what they are doing. We can't avoid having ministry time because Jesus said, "As you go, proclaim this message: 'The kingdom of heaven has come near.' Heal the sick, raise the dead, cleanse those who have leprosy, drive out demons" (Matt 10:7-8). However, we shouldn't harm people because as Jesus said we must, "Love your neighbor as yourself" (Matt 19:19). Therefore, we must learn to lead ministry time in a way that minimizes the potential dangers and maximizes God's ability to do what He wants.

The most helpful way I have found to do that is by thinking about ministry time on two continuums. The first continuum deals with power. The second continuum deals with healthiness.

Powerful Ministry Time

Powerful ministry time happens when God brings his Kingdom. Sometimes He heals people instantaneously, sometimes He drives out demons, and at other times He gives life-altering prophetic words.

But don't confuse powerful ministry time with dramatic ministry time. For example, God may simply send His Spirit of peace. Peace is powerful. We know that peace that passes all understanding (Phil 4:7) is an element of the Kingdom, but it's not necessarily dramatic in its appearance. God may also speak through a scripture. When God is highlighting a passage, it can pierce the heart like a sword, but it's not dramatic.

Also, be wary of losing your expectation for the dramatic. With God all things are possible, and He loves to show off.

The measure of the power of ministry time is not 'what happens' but rather, 'is God in it?' Those who chase the dramatic will end up missing out on certain elements of God's power, as will those who avoid it.

Powerless Ministry Time

Powerless ministry time is when we set aside time for ministry, but it seems like God isn't involved. Most people chalk the experience up to God being silent or distant. However, the real reason is typically a people problem. Jesus taught, "The Father is always working (John 5:17)." If He's always at work, then we are probably missing what He's doing if nothing happens. We will delve more into this later, but suffice to say He is never the problem.

Healthy Ministry Time

When something is healthy, it is life giving. Jesus said that He came to bring life (John 6:33). Therefore, healthiness in a ministry time context is a characteristic of being in right relationship with God, people, the Bible, and ourselves. That's when we are the most alive. When this happens, ministry time draws people to God and expresses His unconditional love. It is authentic and free from unnecessary hype and pretense. Everyone is treated with honor and dignity, and we are challenged to grow in our faith. People are free to take risks, celebrated when they succeed, and encouraged to keep trying when they fail. Scripture is valued, while wisdom and spiritual discernment are honored. The Spirit is free to do whatever He chooses, any way He chooses to do it. God's will is done God's way with God's heart. Believers practice supernatural rest and dependence on the Lord as they pray.

Unhealthy Ministry Time

Unhealthy ministry time can destroy people. It pushes them away from God, and can make them feel too guilty or ashamed to possibly be loved by Him. It can be filled with manipulation and deceit, and often over sells, and under delivers. It disregards the clear teachings of scripture and spiritual discernment. The Spirit is quenched, man's will is done in God's name, or there is striving to manipulate God to do our bidding.

The Grid

Every time you lead ministry time it will end up somewhere on this grid.

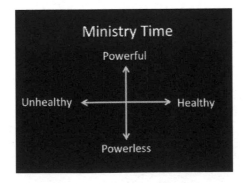

Powerful and Unhealthy

Some groups pursue the Spirit but with bad theology and without concern for maintaining healthy relationships. Their mindset is that if God is showing up, then it doesn't matter what they say, or how they do things. They see God show up in really big ways, but they leave a trail of burnt people in their wake, such as what happened with my friend who's faith was blamed for his girlfriend's death. These groups ministry times are powerful, but harmful.

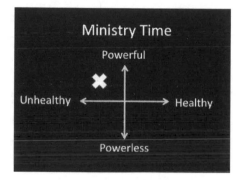

Others choose safety at all costs. These groups are typically comprised of people who have never been taught how to follow the Spirit, or of those who've been burnt by the wild and reckless. They believe God can move, but they are too afraid to step out boldly because they might hurt someone or be hurt themselves. This holds the kingdom back, and keeps them from knowing the power of the Spirit.

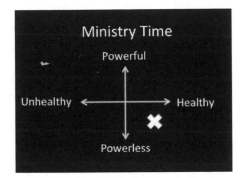

Sadly, most groups fall into one of these two categories, and both approaches fall short of God's desire. Harming people is equally wrong as quenching the Spirit. Thankfully, there is a radical middle. We can learn to follow the Spirit and build people up every time we lead. The church must learn the art of powerful and healthy ministry time. But how?

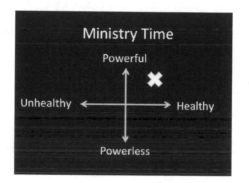

The goal of this book is to answer that very question. It is designed to develop church leaders at every level into mature ministry time coaches. I have found that the reason most churches don't have healthy and powerful ministry time is because leaders are not taught how to do it.

The first part of the book will cover coaching in a small group. If you are a senior leader, I suggest you start by learning in a home group, and not the pulpit. The principles are the same for both environments, however, the larger the group the more likely a mistake is to cause greater harm. Secondly, if you are uncomfortable leading ministry in a small group, what makes you think that you will lead well up front?

Note:

This book assumes that you have had training on the theology of the kingdom, hearing God's voice, the prophetic, physical healing, inner healing, and deliverance. So I will not address them. If you would like to learn more about those subjects, visit my site SimplyKingdom.com.

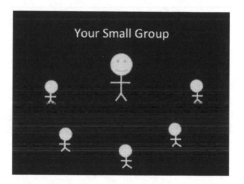

WHAT'S THE POINT?

The people in your group live busy lives, and often come to small group thinking about their needs. Some have health issues, and others might have financial problems. Some need inner healing, and others are worried about their kids.

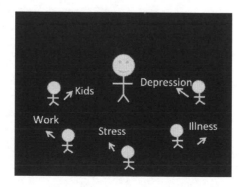

If I told you that you had to lead your small group in ministry time, and you had never done it before, you might have a lot of questions. Most people do. I know I did.

Do I just ask the group who needs prayer and go from there? Do I choose the person with the most needs or do I pick the person with the easiest problem to handle? Does a certain type of prayer bring God's power? What role does faith play? What if someone does something weird? What if they say something hurtful? What if someone is shaking and I don't know if it's God, the demonic, or just their personality manifesting?

I will address these questions shortly, but the most important question is, "How do I define success in ministry time?" In order to have any chance of being successful at anything in life you must clearly define what you intend to accomplish. Andy Stanley calls this "defining the win."

On a baseball team every player knows they win by scoring more runs than the other team. But what about ministry time, what's the win in that arena?

There are good things that look like they could be "wins" but they are not. I played high school basketball with a guy whose personal win was to score as many points as he could. Scoring points is normally a good thing, but he took shoots he shouldn't have taken. The guy scored a lot of points to reach his goal, but the team would have scored more had he passed the ball. In fact, we lost many games because of his need to be the team's MVP. His choice for his personal win kept the team from winning.

Ministry time often becomes unhealthy because well-intentioned leaders choose the wrong win. They see things that are good, and make them the goal. This turns ministry time into something God didn't create it to be. If we have the wrong win, we either we go home feeling like losers, or we have to do something to make it seem like God is at work in order to reach our goal, which usually leaves people harmed.

For some, their win is to get everyone who has never spoken in tongues to do so. Speaking in tongues is a good thing; Paul wished that we all spoke in tongues (1 Cor. 14:5). But is getting people to speak in tongues the point of ministry time? What if the Spirit wants to do something else? If that's the case, either nothing will happen, or the leader will end up pressuring people in order to get their desired win.

The same thing happens when a leader defines being slain in the Spirit, or getting people drunk in the Spirit, as success. I have been shaken to the ground by the power of God. After I got up, I had a renewed love for Jesus. Alternatively, I have also been in a church where everyone was expected to fall backwards because the leader defined that as win for ministry time. It felt fraudulent, and I felt ashamed for being in the crowd, afraid that it might damage a younger believer's faith. We don't have to fake God's power. When He shows up, it's clear.

I knew a person whose win was to see healings. He would tell every sick person he knew that "Jesus is going to heal you when I pray for you." He knew there was a high correlation between faith and healing, and it worked. Some people got healed from his prayer, but others didn't. So he essentially lied to them. What do you think those people thought afterwards? Jesus is supposed to heal me, but He didn't heal me. Did Jesus or did that guy lie to me? Can I trust Jesus, or is it Christians that I need to be skeptical about?

As a younger pastor, I felt like a failure because my win was to have exciting stories. I went home feeling like a loser if something dramatic didn't happen. It created pressure in me to perform. I even knew some ministers who took things a bit farther. They intentionally left details out of testimonies in order to make them grander. Some went as far as to falsify details, or use social pressure to make people tell them what they wanted to hear.

After seeing the affects that having the wrong win can have on people's lives, I got really serious about discovering God's win for ministry time. How does He measure success? After a period of reading the scriptures, prayer, and deep reflection, I discovered what I now view to be God's definition of success through the life of Jesus.

Jesus dealt with the same issues we face. He was surrounded by needs just like us, yet He consistently saw the Father meet people's needs.

You may be thinking, "But Jesus was God in the flesh." He was. However, Jesus came to earth choosing to live life as a human in right relationship to the Father would, which is why He said, "I tell you the truth, the Son can do nothing by Himself" (John 5:19). Nothing signifies that He did not rely on His own power, but depended on His Father to preform miracles. Jesus went on to say, "He can do only what He sees His Father doing, because whatever the Father does the Son also does" (John 5:19).

In this text, Jesus answers the questions: "Where do I begin," and, "What must I do to see power?" We must begin by discovering what the Father is doing because He is the source of power.

The Father is always at work bringing the kingdom to Earth. He is always drawing people to Himself, healing, and setting people free.

Jesus didn't bother thinking up good ideas about how to bring the kingdom. Instead, He focused on discovering what His Father was doing at that moment. Jesus would ask, "Father, what are you doing now?" The Father would reveal how He was working, and then Jesus would join Him, releasing power.

Not only did Jesus partner with the Father to do ministry, He did it with love, kindness, and compassion. People felt respected, and closer to God after they encountered Him. Studying the life of Jesus led me to conclude that the win for ministry time is to do what God is doing in a healthy way.

Most people in your group don't know what the "win" is for ministry time, so they make up their own. When people don't know what to do, they will do what they think is best. One person might choose to make their win getting everybody to pray in tongues. Another might make the win making everyone prophesy.

This is why ministry time often seems so chaotic. There may be people in your group trying to accomplish ten different wins. Chaos is an environment where people get harmed; it is like everyone in the same gym playing a different sport. It's an accident waiting to happen.

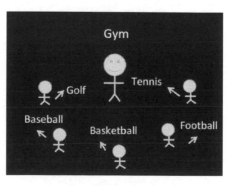

Your job is to simply lead your group to transition from focusing on themselves to focusing on what the Lord is doing, and join with Him in a healthy way.

When a leader makes room for God to lead, He actually will. Jesus is the head of the church, and His job is to lead it (Col 1:18-20). A church leader's job is to make sure that Jesus is free to do His job. Those roles often get reversed. Some think that their job is to lead, and Jesus' job is to bless what they've chosen to do. Jesus will not force us to let Him lead. We have the power to choose to do our own thing, and He will let us do it for as long as we want. However, when we give control to Jesus, He shows up to do powerful things. Ministry time becomes easier because of the power of His presence. When Jesus is in control of the church, He ministers where He sees fit. The gifts are given <u>from</u> Jesus <u>through</u> people as they minister to others.

A Glimpse

The message of this chapter has been that God's power can be released when the body is unified around His heart. Jesus sought an intimate understanding of what His Father was doing as the source of His power for ministry. When we do the same, Jesus takes the lead in our ministry. Everyone participates as a team, empowered by His gifts, and individuals are able to grow in a comfortable learning environment unencumbered by the pressure to perform. To illustrate how this happens in small groups, not just the pages of a book, I'd like to tell you a story about a small group I led.

On this particular occasion, I opened ministry time by coaching my group to focus on the Lord. I asked the Spirit to minister, and after three or four minutes of silence, God gave my wife, Alison, a word of knowledge that someone had knee problems. Joe, a repairman, raised his hand in response to the word of knowledge, telling us that it was for his knees. We all gathered around him and placed our hands on him. A man named John gave another prophetic word about seeing little crystal balls in Joe's knees. As a team we began to pray what John had revealed; "God make the crystal balls in Joe's knees dissolve." Alison felt that God wanted her to sing a worship song in order to release His power. She sang "Come, Lord Jesus, Come" while a man named Wade went off to the side to intercede. I felt led to tell Joe, "Sometimes God heals us when we check things out as an act of faith." Joe began squatting up and down, but the movement still hurt. We prayed for a little while longer, but nothing seemed to be happening. In the end, I released a blessing over Joe, praying that he would experience God's love. I always want people to walk away from healing prayer feeling love regardless of whether or not a miracle occurs.

After the prayer of blessing, Joe said, "I feel a strange heat in my back. Does that mean anything?" He went on to explain that he had back problems as well. I said, "That is probably God at work in your back. Let's pray for it." Ester began to cry; the gift of compassion was in her heart. When I saw her gift emerging, I got excited—I was recalling that Jesus would weep for the masses before He healed them. However, I could tell Ester was timid, so I placed her hands on Joe's back, and prayed, "God, your presence is on Ester, help her to pray your words." She prayed one of the most powerful and beautiful prayers. When she finished, we asked Joe to check out his back by moving in a way that had caused pain before. That day, he was completely healed of the pain.

God used everyone in different ways and roles that day. He personally organized the entire prayer time. We didn't have to take prayer requests or make an order of service, only make ourselves available to the Father's purposes as Jesus did. As you read the following chapters on small group leadership, there may seem like there is a lot to learn. However, remember that Jesus loves using His whole church to do ministry time.

WHAT'S MY ROLE?

When your small group focuses on "the win", a powerful social dynamic takes place: they become a team. A team is a group of people with different gifts and roles who come together to accomplish the same goal. Healthy ministry time is a product of everyone in the group working together. With that said, I have found that there are four roles that emerge.

Prayer Minister

The prayer minister is the person God is currently using to pray. Their role is to do what the Father is doing in a healthy way.

Receiver

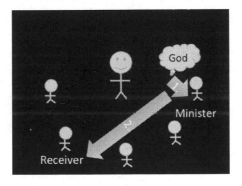

The receiver is the person receiving ministry; their job is fairly simple - rest and let God do whatever He wants. Sometimes your group will not have a receiver.

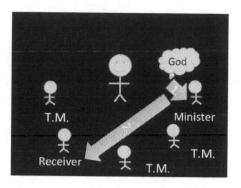

If someone is not ministering or receiving prayer, there is still work for them to do. The teammates are there for support. They are interceding and listening to God while the minister is praying.

Coach

The leader in the group is the coach. The coach's job is to develop a winning team. Some coaches fail at their job because they spend most of their time trying to do the prayer minister's job or do God's job. God's job is to do miracles, the prayer minister's job is to pray, and the coach's job is to develop people (Matt 28:18-20).

Developing people is accomplished by training them through creating and facilitating a healthy environment for them to grow in while doing ministry.

Jesus has placed you in a leadership position for a reason. He expects all of his leaders to build up the body (Eph. 4:11-12). There are not two classes of leaders: the superstars who do ministry time, or the "average people," who don't have to lead. You may have never seen a miracle, or prayed in public, but now it is your job to equip His people because you are their small group leader. It is of absolute importance that you own this and take responsibility for it. His people either will thrive or stay stagnant in part as a result of the way you coach.

Power and Responsibility

Jesus has given us great influence over people's lives. As Voltaire once said, "with great power comes great responsibility." The world uses its power for its own benefit, but God wants us to use that power to benefit those we serve by empowering them. He has placed gifts in them that need to be encouraged and cultivated.

A prayer minister is empowered when they can do healthy and powerful ministry successfully without a leader around, and when his or her testimonies are bigger than their teachers. If you are not empowering people, you are abusing your spiritual authority.

Empowering is about being a spiritual father or mother. A parent gives their kids everything they have without expectations of being repaid. It's what Jesus did for us. You may be saying, "I don't have a lot to give," but as one church leader said: "The goal is not to fill someone else's cup, but to empty your own."

This is not about replicating yourself in someone else. Rather it is about giving the next generation of believers something in order to build something better. Your goal should be that your ceiling will be their floor.

God has intentionally placed you in the position you are in now. You have influence, and you need to own it. It's only when you own it that you will be able to use your influence for the good He has intended. You are their coach, and as their coach, you must draw out the greatness in them that God has put there. What God wants to do transcends yourself. It's not about you; it's about glorifying Jesus and expanding His kingdom by developing others.

FACILITATING MINISTRY TIME

Facilitating ministry time is simply setting your group up to win. When I lead a small group, I structure everything I do around the win. If something will help people do what the Father is doing in a healthy way, then I will add it; if it distracts from that, then I will eliminate it.

However, my way is not "The Way." "The Way" is Jesus. Over time He will guide you and show you things to add or change. If you are new to this, it may be best to simply copy what I have learned and slowly make changes to fit your own style.

Every coach knows that if you don't make time to practice, your team will not develop the skills to win. I recommend scheduling time to practice praying for each other. Too often small group leaders leave only five minutes for prayer. That's not enough time.

Paul refers to the Holy Spirit as a fire that can be quenched or fanned. "Do not put out the Spirit's fire" (1 Thes. 5:19). Fan the flame of the gift of God, which is in you" (2 Tim 1:6). A fire needs certain things to live and grow: oxygen, fuel, and heat. If you remove one of these elements, the fire will die; if you increase these elements, it will grow larger and hotter than before.

Time is to the Holy Spirit's ministry as oxygen is to a fire. It is invisible, but essential. The number one reason the Spirit is quenched in the church is because we do not make time for Him. Of course, there is a huge difference between giving the Holy Spirit 30 seconds in a meeting or 45 minutes. If you want to see Him move, you will have to intentionally carve out longer time periods. I recommend at least 20-30 minutes every small group.

Setting the Room up to Win

Every environment communicates something. Before people arrive, I like to arrange chairs in a circle because it communicates that we are a team, and everyone is invited to participate. When people sit in a semicircle, they step out less because they will expect the leader to do the ministry. Why? The room is set up like a theater. In a theater, only the performers on stage get to interact. A circle invites people interact. Your team can't win if your group is not participating.

Making Time For People to Reconnect

People need to reconnect with their friends. If you don't make time for connection at the beginning of the meeting, people will use ministry time for connecting which will be a distraction.

To help make things comfortable, I provide snacks, and allow 20 minutes at the beginning of every group to give people time to connect. This also allows late comers time to arrive without interrupting the small group.

Share Testimonies

I like to start groups by asking for testimonies. I love to hear where God is at work in people's lives. Testimonies build people's faith, creates hunger, and fosters a culture of expectation. Bill Johnson once said, "When people tell testimonies, their faith and expectations increase. When their faith and expectation increases, they are more likely to step out. When they step out they are more likely to see miracles. When people stop hearing testimonies, they forget how powerful God is, so their expectation decreases and so they stop stepping out. Because they stop stepping out, they stop seeing miracles."

I have three rules when it comes to sharing testimonies. The first it to make them brief, lasting less than 45 seconds. If you tell people to keep them less than a minute, that can mean anywhere from 60 seconds to 10 minutes in people's minds. If more details are needed, then you can ask more questions.

My second rule is to make Jesus the hero. We should boast in the Lord and give Him the glory. There is a big difference between, "I prayed for Jim and he was healed," and, "I prayed for Jim and Jesus healed him." The difference is who's the hero.

Lastly, the testimonies need to convey what really happened. Sometimes people like to leave out or add details to make things more exciting. It works for the sake of exciting storytelling but the problem comes when people start checking into things. If you haven't been as truthful as possible, people will start to doubt ministry time as a whole.

Worship

There is a deep connection that can only happens during longer worship sessions. I think that longer worship sessions every few weeks can be more powerful than doing a session every week that feels cut short. It is very hard to have teaching, extended worship, and ministry time in the same week, so consider doing one or two every other week. Do not go long periods of time without worshiping in your group.

Some worship leaders flow in the Spirit, and some do not. Try to get those who do, even if you have to invite someone in from outside of the group.

Worship can set the atmosphere for ministry time, yet it can also kill the atmosphere if it is not Spirit led. Use CDs if you have to. Most people are more forgiving when you use good CDs rather than having a bad worship leader. Just because someone can play and sing does not mean they should lead worship in your group.

If you use CDs, try to turn up the music really loud so that people cannot hear themselves sing. This will make them feel comfortable singing knowing others can't hear them. Choose songs your church sings on Sunday morning so that everyone will know them.

Also, ask everyone to stand up for at least the first few songs. If they sit, they might not engage with worship as much. Simply doing this usually makes the difference between having people raise their hands and dance, or staring at the floor barely mouthing words.

Working with a Musician

Always have a conversation with your musician beforehand about your expectations for worship. If you do not, transitions can be awkward. If this is your first time working with someone, try to touch base a few days before so that they can prepare.

A musician will need to know the general time frame for how long you want them to lead. It's best to let them pick the songs to allow them to play what they know, but ask them to steer toward songs everyone knows.

Encourage them to pray and let the Spirit lead. If you don't have this discussion, they might not follow the Spirit's leading to honor the time frame you gave them.

Sometimes worship leaders can go too long, therefore discuss hand signals that communicate to keep going, wrap it up, repeat that phrase, etc. Sometimes the worship leader will miss the signals. When this happens simply wait for an interlude, and start speaking or praying. No one will know, and the leader will get the hint. Be sure also to discuss whether or not you want them to play background music during ministry time. Music can be very helpful during ministry time, but depending on instruments being used, a player's fingers can start hurting after a while. Do not to turn worship into a formula in order to get God to come. That is manipulation.

I worked with an anointed worship leader who listened to the Spirit. She would worship during ministry time as the Spirit led, sometimes simply in prayer for the whole time and at other times singing a completely new song the Spirit gave her. She would start to sing, and the group would join in. Secondly, you do not need worship to lead ministry time. Most of the time I lead ministry without it.

After worship I would typically teach on something, and then transition to ministry time.

Creating a Safe Environment Through Boundaries

Coaches know that injuries keep teams from winning; that's why their first concern is safety. Football coaches make players practice in pads, and set up boundaries for what to do and not do.

Ministry time can be messy. People are going to get hurt, but some of these wounds are needless and can be minimized and even prevented. The first time you lead in a new group, you need to make your boundaries clear. It's best to do this after teaching rather than during ministry time, so that it will not distract people from God.

You create a healthy environment by setting boundaries in the group and enforcing them. Healthy boundaries protect people and the flow of the Spirit without quenching or inhibiting Him.
The following are boundaries that I have found effective:

- No one is to be disrespected. If someone has something to say that may come across as painful, then say it in the gentlest way possible.
- Prophetic words must be edifying, comforting and consoling. Focus on calling out the gold vs. focusing on the sin.
- Don't give explanations for why God didn't do something, like heal a sick person. Call it a mystery.
- Avoid unnecessary talking and advice giving during ministry time.

Advice giving is a vice when it comes to ministry time. Nothing can quench the Spirit like a prolonged advice giving-a-thon. When one person shares advice, it triggers thoughts in another to share, and then another. Before long ten minutes have gone by, while people have stopped focusing on God. I have had powerful encounters with God and later forgot what He said because I was being smothered by advice.

If someone needs advice, direct that person to ask God for it. His advice is dead on and they are more likely to receive correction from God as opposed to others. There are times when God gives someone advice to share, but it should only take a moment, and be encased in a "I feel God saying" sentence (if and only if that is what they truly feel the Spirit is saying). If someone absolutely has to share advice, tell them to wait until debrief time or until after the meeting. If it's important, they will remember it.

A church's senior leadership must define their boundaries in the following areas. What should happen if someone has a prophetic word about the recovery of a dying relative, a future spouse, future children, or a correctional word like, "stop looking at porn," or a directional word like telling someone to go to China? These types of words have the potential for being either beneficial or damaging. Some churches allow them, others don't, and others only allow mature prophetic people to give them. Find out from your church's leadership what they want, and honor that within your group.

Lastly, rules are different from boundaries. Rules say do not do X, whereas boundaries have consequences for crossing them. If someone crosses a boundary, at a minimum, you should correct them on the spot or shortly after, and give them a positive alternative. You might say, "I cannot allow people to be disrespected. Will you think of a kinder way to say that?" If the person pushes back, then give them a choice: "You can either comply or choose to be silent. Which do you choose?" Don't use boundaries to punish or restrict other's freedom -- that's not their purpose. Boundaries are made to keep things safe.

Write out your boundaries and give them to the group. Keep the list short. If it's more than 5-7 boundaries, people may forget.

There will be times where you will have to set boundaries beyond what you have written to protect the group. However, one of the biggest mistakes I see happen is that a leader will set up boundaries to deal with the problems caused by a single individual. This will often end up hindering the group and quenching the Spirit. Set individual boundaries for problematic individuals. Leaders often avoid dealing with problematic individuals by setting rules for the entire group. Leaders fall into this when they have a fear of people or have a tendency to avoid conflict or confrontation. This sets the group up to fail because the additional rules aren't needed for everyone and hinders them.

Restating the Win

At some point you will transition to ministry time. This can be at any point depending on what the Spirit is doing. The best thing a leader can do to set their group up for healthy and powerful ministry time is to begin by stating the win. The group may know what the win is, but that doesn't mean that they are focusing on God at the moment.

So when I lead I say something along the lines of, "What we are about to do is set aside our own agendas and focus on what God wants to do. Our only goal is to find out where He is working and do what He wants to do in a healthy way. Sometimes God speaks by bringing a phrase or picture into the movie screen of your mind. If you are not sure if something is from God or not, share it with the group. We are here to help each other. Remember, we want to make ministry time sacred so no advice giving until the debrief time."

I say something like this every time I lead. The words change, but the message stays the same. Stating "the win" is a simple and powerful tool. It's a short opening message that defines what ministry time is and is not for your group. It communicates that your small group is a time to focus on God, and to co-labor with Him, it's not a group counseling session or a chat room. This helps new people know readily how to get involved and that they have your permission to step out in the Spirit, while relieving them from any pressure to perform. Stating "the win" keeps people from trying to do the Holy Spirit's job, or expecting Him to do their job. Finally, it keeps people from trying to repeat a spiritual experience that they once had.

Also, you will set a standard by which the group measures success, so that afterwards you can check to see if you won. Did you seek to find out where God was working or did you do something else? Did you do things in a healthy way or is there something you need to work on?

Over time the win will become a part of your group's culture. Everyone will know it, and start to live it. They will teach it to the guests they invite. It will be tempting to stop stating the win. However, don't stop, or your group will start to drift over time. Once a group drifts, it can be hard to get them back on course. Lastly, I find it safe to assume there might be one person who is not focused. Repetition will help them get back on track, even if they know what they should be doing.

Dialing Down

Dialing down is the process of setting aside distractions in order to connect with God. It's an intentional process. People rarely dial down without making an effort to do so. So at first you are going to have to walk a new group through it each time until it becomes natural for them to do it on their own.

You might say something like, "Let's just take a moment to set our agendas aside. Intentionally let your thoughts go. You don't need to worry about what should or should not happen. This is God's time. Give it to Him. Let's turn our attention to Jesus."

Inviting God

Next, invite God to direct the group. Keep it short and sweet. The words you use don't matter, it's your relationship with God that matters. Jesus died for you, you are now His child, and when you pray He hears it. He is always at work, and He will reveal where He wants to work to someone in the group.

You might say something like, "God, help us connect with You tonight. Show us where to begin. We want to see the kingdom come. Heal the sick, set people free, draw people back to You, and change our hearts. Lead this time, Father."

When I invite God, I know that He will move in the same way that I know the sun will rise in the morning. How can I know this? Because He is good and always faithful. He is always present and always at work. Believing these things is a choice you make. There is something about being confident in what Jesus' death and resurrection have done for your relationship with God that releases the kingdom.

Also, I don't ask for prayer requests before ministry time. In my opinion, they eat up too much time. Often people will share for 20 minutes, leaving only 10 minutes to pray. Typically, the prayer requests will be covered through prophetic words. Occasionally, I will ask for prayer requests if there is a lull about two thirds of the way through. If someone needs prayer or has a prayer request that's really urgent, they will bring it up.

Waiting

After you pray, your job is done. Now it's God's turn. The Scriptures say, "Wait for the LORD; be strong and take heart and wait for the LORD" (Psalm 27:14). When you wait, remain in silence for God to reveal where He wants to begin.

The key word here is silence. As much as waiting in silence is the easiest thing to do for some, it's can also be the most difficult thing to do for others. People's emotions are going to be screaming to do something else. Many Christians have never had to depend on God before, therefore the rawness of trusting God can make people anxious.

Coaching People While They Wait

When people are first learning to wait, they tend to get distracted easily. Every 30 seconds or so I will coach them back to the task of listening.

"As you wait, distracting thoughts might enter your into mind. Just set them aside."

(30-45 seconds goes by.)

"God speaks many times by causing a thought to "pop" into someone's mind. In light of this, you should not be straining to hear God's voice. "

Pause again for some time.

"If you think you have a word, but you are not sure if it's God or not, just share it with the group and we can check it out. We all want to hear from God, and no one is going to judge you if you miss it. We are all here to learn."

Also, things might pop into someone's head while they are dialing down. Sometimes it is feelings of inadequacy, restlessness, or just the awkwardness of the situation. Sometimes it is lies that they believe. Be sure to address these by saying something like this:

"Maybe you are feeling a little weird. Maybe you are scared of what might happen. Why don't you just give that to God right now?"

Helping with Transitions

Eventually someone will get a direction such as a song, a scripture, or a word of knowledge. They might begin to pray for someone, and then another member might join in to pray for that same person. Eventually, you will sense that the Spirit's ministry with that person is complete. New groups will not know what to do next, so walk them through dialing down again.

"We thank you Lord for what you just did. Do you want to work anywhere else? Let's refocus on listening."

Part of your job as a coach is to make prayer ministry more fluid. A coach is like a tour guide, taking the group through the process, explaining what is significant, and moving the group smoothly to the next point of interest. When the group gets stuck, coach them out of it. Sometimes a person will get a word of knowledge for a person. For example, "I feel like God is saying someone in the room has unforgiveness toward their dad." The person who got the word may not know how to transition that into ministry. Help them by asking the group, "Does anyone have unforgiveness?" If the answer is yes, then have the person who got the word pray for the individual the word was for.

Sometimes the word is only a picture, but the person who got it doesn't know what it means. Therefore, they will not know what to do next. When that happens, ask God to give the group the interpretation.

Some people need a nudge to step out. On occasion, I will ask a shy person to pray for someone in the group. Be aware of those who are introverted or shy as many are quite gifted and are simply waiting for someone to see their gifts and give them permission to express themselves.

Everyone has a box that they feel comfortable ministering in. You will notice at times that your group is pressing into something and they need to push outside of their box. In one of my groups, a person was praying for God to touch the group. He was praying bold things, but he was whispering. A group member said, "Push through. You are dead on, but put your heart into it." That gave the man courage and freedom, and when he prayed the Spirit fell.

Other times the group will want to move on from a topic when the Spirit isn't finished in an area. You will have to encourage the group to refocus on the issue. I will use my friend, Chris, as an amazing example for how to do this. One Sunday, a thirty year old man came forward with his daughter to the prayer team to get prayer for his shingles. He was so sick he had to use a walker. The prayer team prayed for him, and prayed again. Nothing happened. The team gave up and started talking but then Chris said, "We are not done here. Let's pray again." It is a very bold faith-filled act to call others back to prayer when they have given up. However, after two or three other rounds of prayer, the man was healed and walked out of the service carrying his little girl.

I know a girl who prayed for a man on the streets seven times before she saw healing. Imagine how awkward it is after the sixth failed prayer to ask, "Can I pray for you once more?" If something in your gut tells you to keep praying, then do it. Our human tendency is to follow the crowd so if something is telling you to keep praying, it is probably the Holy Spirit.

I have been in groups where the coach didn't help the group make transitions. It was really awkward because the leader wasn't leading. Most people appreciate it when you help things keep flowing.

There are no formulas for how an evening should go. Some weeks the Spirit will lead your group to pray for the local church, other times toward inner healing and deliverance, other times to pray for a sick person, give prophetic words, or go to the streets.

Debriefing

When ministry time is over, take time to debrief. Debriefing allows people to process what happened. It is best to start off with a positive testimony, so ask the group to share about something God did. Then ask questions that could bring to light issues people are wondering about.

"Did anyone learn anything?"

"Where do we need to grow as a group?"

"Does anyone want to talk about what happened?"

Sometimes, if something really unusual happens, like a demonic manifestation, it is best to skip to debriefing, after your group has taken care of it.

After Group

Plan to stay about 15-20 minutes after group. I make an effort to ask new people what their experience was like. I also use that time to have one-on-ones with people. If you want people to grow, you are going to have to pastor them. Ministry time exponentially increases the amount of effort you are going to have to take to develop people.

Should I Have Direction From God Before We Begin?

Sometimes God gives the leader direction before the group begins, and sometimes He doesn't. It's really important to take the pressure off of yourself to have direction, otherwise you will begin to perform.

Most new leaders lean one of two directions - either they will not listen before their group at all, or they freak out and spend hours trying to hear from God. Which are you more like? My suggestion is to do the opposite of your natural tendency.

Are There Times When I Shouldn't Wait?

There is a difference between practice time and playing the game. During practice, a coach might focus on one area of the game.

For example, a basketball coach might have the players focus on shooting free throws. However, in a game you use the skills you have learned all at once.

Ministry training is like practice, and ministry time is like game day. You need to do both regularly to grow as a group. You also need to clearly communicate to your group when you are doing one or the other, or they will get confused.

When you are training people, you should try to practice what you have taught immediately. If you teach on healing, then have the group pray for the sick. If it's inner healing, then divide the people into groups of twos, and have them practice on each other.

Lastly, there are two things that can hinder individuals when it comes to waiting on God that you should be aware of. First, don't allow the idea of waiting disempower you from doing any ministry at all. When I first began doing ministry, I incorrectly concluded that if God wasn't showing me specific things, He didn't want me to minister to people.

My perspective changed after spending some time with a friend of mine who said something I will never forget: "Unless there's a red light, I have a green light to approach and minister to people. God said "go", and as we go, we'll see where the Father is at work." His insight brought balance to my perspective.

There is a difference between depending on God and codependency with God. When we use waiting as a crutch to keep us from going boldly forward with what He has commissioned us to do in the Bible like evangelism, then we are being codependent.

Secondly, don't confuse your agenda with God's agenda. As much as God will lead us to do things that correspond with the desires of our heart, we must check our motives.

How do I tell the difference between my agenda and God giving me the desire of my heart? I first give the desire to God and then see if it comes back. Secondly, I check my heart to see if I am being driven. For example, do I feel any pressure, expectation, etc. to do something?

If I am not being driven, and the desire returns after giving it to God, then I move forward with doing what I feel led. Setting your agenda aside doesn't mean that your agenda isn't important, it simply means that you are willing to give it up if it is not God's.

Always remember, that God is a good dad, and He doesn't look at your performance, but at your heart. If you want to learn His ways, He will teach you them in a way that is unique to you.

My First Time Leading

I received an invitation from a young woman at our church to teach on prophecy to her college's ministry group. Even though I had never taught before, I decided to go for it.

After I taught the group how to hear God, I paused. I had never been a part of ministry time before, so I wasn't quite sure what to do next. I remembered in a John Wimber tape that he had mentioned circling people up, so I told everyone to get in a circle.

The moment that I had been dreading the past four days was about to happen. I said, "Now I am going to ask God to come and minister to us, and we are going turn this meeting over to Him." I felt a quiver in my voice, as I prayed, "God, we invite you into this place. Let your kingdom come and do signs and wonder among us." Then there was silence. I looked at my watch -- 2:14pm. This was the first time I had ever lead ministry time, and my mind was racing. *What if God doesn't show up? Will these people believe a word I have said?* I had never felt pressure like this before.

Am I anointed enough to be doing this? I had every reason to believe I wasn't. I had never prayed for someone and seen a miracle happen through my own prayers at that point. I was in my first year of ministry as a pastor, and here I was teaching the class because a friend had asked me to.

I looked at my watch again. 2:17, then 2:18, then 2:19. Each minute was growing more and more painful. I began to think, *Maybe I should just make something up, anything is better than this.* It sounds horrible now, but when the adrenaline is rushing, and you are under that kind of pressure, it seemed easier to ask for forgiveness later.

Instead, to break the silence, I started coaching everyone to share anything they thought might be from the Lord, I said something like, "if you get a picture or hear a phrase that might be God, why don't you share it, and let's check it out together. No one is going to judge you if you are wrong." (Because everyone is going to start judging me if nothing happens soon)! 2:20, 2:21. Sweat was pouring down my face, "God get me out of this," I kept praying silently over and over again."

Finally someone spoke up.

"I saw a skateboard fall out of the air and shatter into pieces, and then a lamp fell and did the same thing, and then an apple."

I thought, That sounded really weird. Oh no, what do I do now that someone has given a bad word? No one had ever talked to me about what to do during ministry time. If you are a pastor, you should just know how to do it. I tried to find the words to say, but I was too flustered. Then it occurred to me, maybe we should check the word out.

"Does anyone think this is for them?"

Then someone said, "I think that word is for me. My life feels like it is breaking into a million pieces right now." I told the person who had gotten the word to pray for him. As he prayed, the power of God began to shake the young man's body. When we were done praying, the young man was crying pretty hard. I said, "Thank you God for showing up." I really meant it.

Then everyone looked at me like, "Now what?" I didn't know. Should we stop? Was God done? I had the people dial down again. Nothing was happening. What if the word had been a fluke?

Then someone else got a word. That cycle began to repeat itself throughout the night.

As I drove home, I was exhausted. I felt like I had just run a marathon. That's what your first time may be like; it's always a little scary and surprising. However, always remember that God will show up and cover your weaknesses.

DEALING WITH YOUR FEARS

You must face your fears to coach effectively. Fears are often based on lies, which are misrepresentations of who Jesus is, and who He says you are. To confront a lie you must renew your mind by aligning it with how the Father thinks. When we think as God thinks, we will do what God says. I want to deal with the top four fears that inhibit people from coaching effectively.

I Am Not Anointed

Are you afraid that you might not be spiritual enough to lead ministry time? The truth is you aren't. You'll never have enough faith and you certainly aren't holy enough. Thankfully, Jesus already is those things. It's His work, not yours, that determines your spiritual blessings.

You are in Christ. When the Father sees you, He sees Jesus. You don't become mature enough to lead; you are already anointed to lead because the anointed one lives in you (Eph. 1:14). You were ready before you ever picked up this book. There is nothing you have to do to earn this, and there's nothing you can do to lose this.

The way you fight the lie isn't through reading the Bible more, praying more, or eliminating a secret sin. It's by focusing on Jesus.

The question is, "Where are you going to focus?" Are you going to focus on your faults or on Jesus? It's like looking at the floor and the sky. You can't do both at the same time. Focusing on your shortcomings will always take your eyes off of Him.

What if I Mess Things Up?

Leadership takes all of your issues, puts them on display, and then amplifies them. I have said rude things while correcting people. I have missed the Spirit and as a result I got the group off track. Chances are you will definitely make a mess or two.

However, I have learned Jesus is bigger than any mistakes I make. He works through them. For example, when I had to go back and apologize, my character was strengthened and so were my relationships. He grew me past my fears of admitting I was wrong. I encountered the love of the church and the grace of God in those moments.

He will use your mistakes for your benefit as well. "We know that in all things God works for the good of those who love Him, and have been called according to his purposes" (Rom 8:28).

When they see you have the courage to admit when you are wrong, then it will give them the courage to do the same. When they see that God uses you despite your mistakes, they will begin to believe God can use them that way. God is bigger than we give Him credit for.

What If the People I Lead Make Huge Mistakes?

They will. They will inevitably have bad doctrine, hurt other people, and do something foolish. Some will be offended, and others will get mad. People will leave your church and group because of offenses.

Guess what? If you didn't have ministry time, the same thing would happen. Humans aren't perfect. The only difference is that the churches who implement ministry time experience God's power more frequently.

You can't control people. If you try to control people, you are going to become really bitter as well as angry.

God Might Not Show Up

Many people are afraid of what other people will think of them if they pray and nothing dramatic happens. If you want to become a great leader, you must first decide the role you will allow the opinions of others to play in your life. Listen to what Paul has to say about this:

> "This, then, is how you ought to regard us: as servants of Christ ... Now it is required that those who have been given a trust must prove faithful. I care very little if I am judged by you or by any human court; indeed, I do not even judge myself. .... It is the Lord who judges me" (1 Cor. 4:1-4.).

Paul understood that there is only one opinion that counts, and that there is only one judge who judges justly. So he refused to judge or be judged. Imagine for a moment the freedom you would experience if you did not play the judging game and acknowledged that the Father's opinion is the only one that counts. He does not measure you by your success, but by your faithfulness.

Your job is to abide in Him. His job is to produce the fruit. Obeying God may not always lead to our desired outcomes, but it always lead to an experience with God. You may experience God's power through a miracle, or experience Him as the Comforter when you step out and are disappointed. This forces us to come to terms with our deepest heart issues. Do you value avoiding pain of being judged more than knowing God? The way you live your life will reveal your answer.

DIFFICULT SITUATIONS

This chapter will address some of the challenging situations coaches encounter. My goal is to help you walk through them with honor. In order to navigate difficult issues while respecting others, it is essential for a coach to develop great communication skills.

Dealing with Distractions

New prayer ministers frequently want to chit-chat and give advice. It's easy for them to get distracted. When they do, it is your role to get them back on track. The best way to do this is to restate the win. You might say something like this: "If you have advice to share, please save it for after group. It's important to keep ministry time focused on prayer, so let's refocus on what the Father is doing."

Even when you say it clearly some people might be tempted to add one last comment, and the group might get off track. So after you get done speaking immediately close your eyes. This communicates, "We are done talking. It's time to pray." Most people will stop giving advice because they don't want to interrupt a praying person.

Rambling

Some people ramble. Rambling wastes time. Wasting time keeps the group from winning. Sometimes you will need to address it. One way is to interrupt the rambler, "I'm getting lost, what's your point?"

If the person has a consistent problem with this, meet with them privately after the meeting so you can coach them. People ramble because they don't know what details to leave out of a story. Learning to stop rambling is easy; begin the story by telling the conclusion first. When someone begins with the conclusion first, none of the details are important. If you can help a rambler, you will help transform their relationships.

Correcting Abrasive Comments

Abrasive comments are words that <u>might</u> unnecessarily hurt a healthy person. There will always be people who are unhealthy or overly sensitive, so just focus on addressing comments that would affect a hypothetical person who is in a good place emotionally.

Most of the time when a minister makes abrasive comments, they have good intentions but poor word choices. When correcting someone, you need to give them a reason why you are asking them to change. Example:

"I know your heart was probably in the right place, but that came out a little too abrasive. If someone said that to me, I would probably feel hurt."

Suggest an alternative or ask them how they can communicate the same thing differently next time.

"Do you think that saying _____ would be a kinder way to convey the same message?"

Praying with the Spirit

Every ministry time will have moments when prayer ministers are not praying with the Spirit, and everyone has a moment when they miss it. Although you don't want to draw attention to these times, there are times when this is repeatedly a problem. Then it needs to be addressed. Often this happens when someone doesn't understand the difference between uninhibited prayer and spirit-led prayer. Uninhibited prayer is praying whatever comes to mind, whereas Spirit-led prayer is praying what the Spirit is saying. It takes discernment to tell the difference between the two. Uninhibited prayer is not wrong; in fact, it is usually a sign that a person loves to pray. In order to help uninhibited prayers you have to teach them discernment. You might address it in such a way:

"I love the fact that you love to pray. I'm wondering if you would like a tip on discerning God's voice from your own? When something comes to mind, wait, pay attention to if it keeps coming back to mind. If it does, then it is probably God's voice. Then share."

If the problem persists, have the person wait on sharing until the end of group time. Uninhibited prayer also needs to be stopped when the Spirit is moving in a different direction. Regularly, I experience times when the Spirit's presence is palpable. There is a feeling that at any moment the Holy Spirit is going to move in a dynamic way. All that is needed is for the group to wait a few more seconds. Sometimes uninhibited prayers start occurring, and you can feel the room shift. Let someone know gently that you're going to focus on something else.

"Could you please hold on? I feel like the Spirit is going in a different direction."

People can get insulted when this happens but refrain from having a conversation at that exact moment. If necessary, I might add, "Please trust me on this one, and we can talk after group." Then refocus the group.

Bad Ministry

Sometimes prophecies are wrong. When they are wrong some topics are more explosive than others like whom someone will marry, words of correction, career choices, or subjects regarding life and death. Other times people press inner healing too far and go into issues that the receiver isn't ready to handle. Regardless of the issues, mistakes create messes that have to be cleaned up. The offended person will come to you, expecting you to fix things, and to make up a rule so that it never happens again. Don't do that. Encourage the people to get together and work it out privately. If it can't be resolved between them, then it's time to enter the situation. Before you make any judgment calls hear what everyone has to say.

Lastly, don't make lots of new rules. If you make a rule for every mistake that happens, you will neuter your team. Address the heart issues rather than make a rule to solve a problem. If it is appropriate to make a rule, then create one just for the individual until they have matured. You might say something like, "I need you to come to me first, before you share any more prophetic words so I can discern them before you share. When I think you are ready, I will let you know and we can stop doing this."

Dealing with Unacceptable Theology and Practices

People will often bring their theological backgrounds into the group. Most of the time this isn't a problem because many theological differences don't hinder ministry time. An example of this might be one's views on communion or tithing. However, a belief that healing only comes through placing your faith in God by refusing to take medicine brings a different dynamic to the group. While the group's win is to find out what God is doing, this person might want to manufacture faith. This isn't a problem if he or she is willing to set aside their win during your group's ministry time; the problem happens when there is a war over whose win is right.

The first step is to see if you can, pardon the pun, win your brother or sister over. Have a conversation or two, give away a CD or a book relevant to the topic. Be patient.

However, there are times when theological and methodological conflicts create such a problem that it is harmful to the group, and something has to be done. What should you do? This is when you have a "coming to an understanding" conversation. A "coming to an understanding conversation" is not a theological debate. Theological debates are when two people talk about theology with the hope of winning the other side over. You have already presented your side, and there is no reason to do it again. "Coming to an understanding" is when both parties work to understand how each one thinks, that there is an irresolvable disagreement, and what needs to happen next is communicated. These conversations are best done in private. The first step is to state what you disagree over.

"I love having you in group, but there is something we need to discuss. You and I disagree over how to conduct ministry time because we have different definitions of faith. We could talk until the end of time and neither of us are going to change."

The second step is to state what you will and will not allow in your group.

"This is a (insert church name) small group, and our pastor asked us to do things in a particular way. I know you disagree with that, but I cannot allow what you are doing to happen in this group because I need to honor our pastor's vision for this group."

The third step is to give the person a choice about what to do.

"I need to ask you not to talk about that doctrine in this group. If you feel that you can't, that is understandable. I want for you to feel the freedom to find another group in this city. I'd love for you to stay, but the choice is yours. I just need you to let me know what are you going to do. Which do you choose?"

What happens next is up to them. You have honored them by not trying to control or manipulate him, or avoiding the issues. If they stay, you have protected the group, and if they go, you have protected the group. If you avoid this conversation, you will hinder your group from doing what the Father is doing in a healthy way.

On a side note, there will be people whom you know you need to correct, but are too afraid to bring it up. This is a sign of spiritual idolatry. Coaches must continually strive to stay free from the fear of man and the fear of rejection. All leaders experience moments of unpopularity, but good leaders honor God by making the right choices despite people's opinions of them while maintaining God's heart and godly word choices throughout the process.

Shifting the Atmosphere

An atmosphere is a vibe created by a person's presence. Have you ever been having a great conversation with some friends when a negative person joined the group? After a while the joy seems to disappear. Have you ever noticed that when you are around a really funny person that you will often become funnier? This is because a person's internal state effects group dynamics; they shift the atmosphere of the group.

When people get together in a group, their internal state influences each other, creating an atmosphere. A football game has an atmosphere of excitement, whereas a funeral has an atmosphere of grief.

When your small group gathers together it has its own atmosphere. It is influenced by both human and spiritual beings. One of the keys to leading ministry time is recognizing the atmosphere of the room in any given moment. Is there expectation, fear, faith, judgment, freedom, or skepticism? Throughout the night the atmosphere might change. When I lead I am listening for God's direction as well as feeling the room's atmosphere.

There are atmospheres that are highly correlated with the Kingdom of God coming in power. A small group of people that are filled with faith, expectation, and hunger are highly correlated with seeing the Spirit move. A small group filled with doubt, apathy and skepticism are negatively correlated with seeing the Spirit move.

There is a spiritual battle over which way the atmosphere of your group will shift. When you choose to stand with God, and the atmosphere of a room is not aligned with Him, a tension is created.

A small group leader needs to recognize that standing with Christ will create tensions sometimes. Although you do not control the outcome, you can certainly shape it.

If you notice a negative atmosphere call it out, speak the truth, and pray the opposite. "I feel that there is a lot of doubt and fear in the room tonight, Father, in the name of Jesus I release faith and courage. We choose not to partner with doubt and fear."

You are responsible for your atmosphere. It is not something that happens to you, but rather something you choose to allow to happen, and you can choose to change it. If you blame others, you are not being a responsible leader. One of the enemy's tactics is to make us cave in when we are in atmosphere battles. He knows that if we stand firm then he has to flee.

The Demonic

Sometimes demons will manifest because the presence of God forces them out. You can deal with these manifestations by commanding the demons to go in Jesus' name.

However, you don't have to deal with manifestations if you don't feel you or someone in your group can handle it. It's important to understand that it's not an emergency. You want to use wisdom to take care of that person. First, command the demon to "Stop manifesting in the name of Jesus," and coach the person to take control of their body. No demon has authority to cause an embarrassing scene. Have the afflicted individual call a pastor at the church to set up an appointment.

It's important to convey that demonic manifestations are normal. Say something like, "Tonight was a good reminder that we have a real enemy. Sometimes God reveals demonic strongholds because He wants to set people free. This is normal. John, we want to walk you through the process. It's nothing to be embarrassed about. Many anointed people have had a pest or two to get free from. We don't judge you in any way." This will set the person at rest.

If a demon does manifest, be sure to debrief. As weird as this sounds start by asking, "What positive things happened tonight?" Next, ask if there are any concerns. Don't' allow advice giving to the formally demonized person, or they might feel like a project. Also, be sure to call each group member individually during the week. Demons scare people a lot, and it helps to process their concerns.

When Things get Weird

Ministry time can sometimes be weird. There are several reasons for this. Part of the reason is that people are messy and that makes things weird. Some people are just loud and eccentric, some have personal baggage and poor communication skills. Other times, someone is exaggerating what they are experiencing. However, don't confuse dramatic or loud moves of the Spirit with this type of hype. When the Spirit is moving, you can't shut Him down just because you're trying to prevent hype.

Also, faith itself can be weird. Believing that God can heal cancer makes some people uncomfortable. Not only that, God is intentionally weird. Conrad Gempf, in his book *Jesus Asked*, says that Jesus likes to drive a wedge into the heart of a fence sitter. Lumberjacks use metal wedges to split wood by placing the wedge in the center of the wood with one hand, and then hitting it with a sledgehammer with the other hand. This forces the wood to split apart. God does weird things that force people to make a choice to come closer to Him or reject who He really is.

In John 6, we read about a moment where there was a large crowd following Jesus. He told them that if they wanted any part in Him, they had to eat His flesh and drink His blood. To a Jewish ear it sounded like He was promoting cannibalism.

"On hearing it, many of his disciples said, 'This is a hard teaching. Who can accept it?'" Aware that His disciples were grumbling about this, Jesus said to them, "Does this offend you" (John 6:60-61)?

We must live free from offense. Jesus intentionally offended His disciples to drive a wedge into them. Then Jesus teaches His disciples, "The Spirit gives life; the flesh counts for nothing. The words I have spoken are Spirit and they are life" (John 6:63).

Jesus points out to His disciples that sometimes the Spirit will do things that will offend your mind. This happens to me a lot. There are times when I am praying and I can feel my stomach muscles contracting. I have no clue what is going on, but I know that the Spirit is at work. There are times when people that I have prayed for fell down. "Why did that happen?" they ask. I respond that God did it and when they ask why, all I can say is, "I don't know." If you need an explanation for everything that happens, you may have offense in your heart which needs to be dealt with.

God can be intentionally weird. We can either accept Him on His terms, or be offended and walk away. When God is weird, it's okay. He is God and can do whatever He wants. People can be weird, and that's okay sometimes. But there are going to be times when you will have to stop something. God has called us to be spiritually discerning. The idea that everything is permissible when it is done in the name of the Spirit is false.

There are some big risks associated with stopping something you think may be unhealthy even if you are right. Stopping something offends people. You could cause a bigger distraction, causing people to become more cautious, and to begin questioning themselves. Most importantly, you could be wrong and quench the Spirit.

There have been many times when I was questioning if I should let things slide or not. Then after group someone would say, "This person's prayer ministered to me so much." If possible, that's why I try to wait until after ministry time to discuss things that I am uncertain about.

However, there will be a time when you need to make the call. You are going to start feeling in your gut, *This is really, really weird. Is this God, or should I stop this?*

To help you process how to make the call look at the following scale. On one side is "absolutely sure it is God," and on the other is, "sure it's not God."

Absolutely Sure it's God --------------- Sure it's Not God

Events that trigger your mind to ask, "Should I make the call," will fall somewhere in the middle. You can't figure it out. So what do you do?

Typically what's happening starts to break one way or the other over time. So take your time, and simply watch what is going on for a few moments. God may speak to you or to someone else about what's happening. Also, sometimes things take care of themselves.

If you are becoming increasingly certain that what is happening is not God, then walk over to where the situation is occurring and hover around while observing it. Sometimes your presence will alert the prayer minister that something is going wrong, and they will correct it without you having to say something.

If you are still not sure, but you are finding yourself increasingly worried, then ask the prayer minister, "Can you help me understand what's happening here?" Let them explain. If you are not sure if it's God, leave it alone.

However, there comes a point when you know you have to stop what's happening because a deeply held value is being broken. Before you address the issue, you need to take a moment and discover what that value is. Once you know the value being violated and can name it, then speak up.

Start by telling the prayer minister the good that they are doing. The number one area I see coaches fail in correcting people is that they treat mistakes as if everything the prayer minister did was incorrect when it wasn't. Correcting is about encouraging the good and discouraging the bad. If you don't encourage the good, you will eventually end up discouraging it. If you can't come up with anything good, you can say something like, "I love your heart," or, "I love your boldness."

Next, share with the prayer minister the value that you feel is being violated. Stating your value lets the prayer minister know that you don't have a problem with them, but have a different way of seeing the world. Also, state what breaking the value hurts. Every value exists to protect something, and if the prayer minister isn't following that value then something is getting hurt. Then share an alternative behavior that allows them to reach their same goal while complying to your value. This is what it might look like:

"I love your boldness. I can see that you really want to see God move. It is very motivational to me. But every time you pray, you tend to scream a little which hurts my ears. One of our values is being naturally supernatural. We want to minister in a natural tone. Do you think you could keep praying, but this time do it in a natural tone?"

Or,"Gina, I love the fact that you are so open about sharing your problems. However, John is not here to state his side of the story. One of our values is honor and respect. I think that continuing to share would be dishonoring to him. Why don't you and I plan on going to talk to him this next week, and we can pray for your heart right now?"

Which situations occur most frequently for you? What is your plan for solving them when they arise again? Talk with your small group coach about this.

TRAINING

The first day of little league practice the coach sat us down and taught us the game. "This is how to hold the ball. This is how you swing a bat. This is the direction you run around the bases. These are the rules." I was glad he did because I didn't know how to play baseball. He was training us.

Training is teaching people how to win, telling them what to do, letting them do it, and giving them feedback to develop their strengths.

Imagine what would have happened if the coach assumed everyone knew how to play baseball. I would have never learned. This is what happens in most churches. One of the reasons the Spirit is quenched in the church is because leaders fail to teach people the basics of prayer ministry, such as spending time with Jesus, hearing God, prophecy, praying for healing, inner healing, and deliverance.

If you find yourself training a group, and don't feel like you have mastered the basics yet, don't worry. One of the bests way to learn them is to teach others. Read a good book like *Empowered Evangelicals* by Rich Nathan, and then step out. That being said, you are not always going to have a small group that is focused on teaching about the spiritual gifts. For example, you might lead a group on managing your money. In order to be effective in teaching time, you will have to devote your time to that. So when you don't have an hour to teach on the gifts, you can use something called spot coaching.

Spot Coaching

Spot coaching is simply taking 45 seconds to explain a topic of prayer ministry, and then doing it as a team. It's very effective because people learn more from doing something than from hearing about it. Here is an example of spot coaching for healing: "We are about to pray for the sick. It's important to understand that sometimes people get healed when we pray for them. I saw a man who walked with a cane get healed recently. Sometimes people do not get healed. My mother-in-law died of cancer even though we spent an enormous amount of time praying for her. I don't know why. What I do know is that God wants us to pray for sick people. When you pray for a sick person, interview them first. Find out what's wrong by asking, 'What do you want Jesus to heal? Do you have any pain now? On a scale of 0-10 how much pain do you have?'

Get them to show you what they can and cannot do. 'How high can you lift your leg?' Then pray a Spirit led prayer. Keep your eyes open. Once you've stopped praying, assess the situation. "Are you feeling anything?' If they need more prayer and will allow you to continue, keep going. Stop when they are healed, or when person you are praying for doesn't want more prayer, or when the Spirit's done, or whenever you're done. If they have questions, answer them. Don't try to work your emotions or faith up. Just let God be God, and trust the Spirit. Also, sometimes it is best to command the affliction to leave." Once you've said what you need to say, let the group loose. They will be nearly as effective from a 45 second talk, as they will from a 45 minute talk. The secret to helping people learn through spot coaching is knowing exactly what you need to communicate about a topic and using repetition. You want to say the same thing over and over again each week so that people can pick up the details.

Spot coaching is effective because it works with how people learn. Traditional teaching says that a person should be taught everything about a topic, memorize all that's been taught, and then do everything that needs to be done from the memory for the rest of one's life. No one learns that way.

The way people actually learn is that they will only remember one or two interesting points out of the four or five points that are being taught. Then while they begin to pray, questions will naturally emerge. The next time you spot coach, the questions will be in their minds, and they might remember point 4 because it answers their question. They will now apply it. They will have more questions to be answered and will remember them the next time you spot coach. Experience is always the best teacher.

Also, throughout ministry time I give feedback as needed. Most feedback is only ten seconds. For example, you might say, "Be sure to ask if you can place your hands on him before you pray. Don't assume. If someone has been abused, that might be a trigger point for them." I have found that most people really value feedback.

Practice

Knowing how to throw a baseball straight is not the same as being able to throw a baseball straight. I can teach you how to hold a baseball in two seconds. It takes years to develop a throwing arm. That requires lots of practice.

Now, imagine a baseball coach that gives his players a stack of books, saying, "Read these and you'll be fine." Next imagine a football coach who spends every practice giving motivational talks with tips on how to play better, and then sends the guys home. Those teams would not perform well. Yet that's what pastors do every week. They tell people what to do, and then tell them to put it into practice themselves.

Prayer ministers are not developed through hearing about how to pray. They have to be developed through practice. In football, great coaches make their teams practice again and again and again and again and again. Day after day, week after week doing the same plays over and over. Frequent practice develops great football players. Likewise, frequent practice develops effective prayer ministers. If you want to develop people who follow the Spirit, you have to create environments for them to practice doing it regularly.

De-lumping

De-lumping is when you break things down into their most basic parts and teach someone to become successful one task at a time. Take for example the process of hearing God and discerning His voice. This is a very complex process that requires a person to learn to wait on God, recognize what He is saying, interpret it, discover the application, and successfully share it with someone. It's so complex that if you expect a group to learn to do everything at once, then they will probably get frustrated and quit. So teach how to hear God in stages (We'll show you how in later chapters).

Regularly Increase Risk

Your group needs to be stretched to grow. There will be times when doing ministry with each other seems routine. There are two things you can do to help stretch them. The first is to bring in a new person with a pressing issue. Don't let the group know why they are there, and see what God does. It's actually easier to get prophetic words for someone who you don't know. In fact, tell the group that they can invite anyone who needs prayer at any time.

Secondly, take your group to the streets. When I do this I don't let the group know it's going to happen. They just come to group, and we divide up into teams. Each one will pray about where to go to minister, and see what happens. Other times we will take up an offering and ask God where He wants us to give the money.

It's best to create roles on each team that require different levels of risk. Some people can stay at the house and pray; others can go and just watch; some might hand out popsicles and clothing. Others will have conversations and pray for people. After I explain the different roles, I tell people to choose one activity that brings them a few degrees out of their comfort zone. This way everyone gets stretched, but not overwhelmed.

Allow People to Experiment

People are not blank slates. God has hardwired them to be a particular way. Each person's hardwiring is different. He intentionally made us the way that we are because He has a purpose that can only be fulfilled in how we are each designed. You have to create an environment where people can discover how they relate to God, and their own ministry style. Your ministry style is not going to be like mine. You and God have to figure that out together.

If you want people to grow you have to create an environment where it is okay to fail. The best gift you can give someone is creating an environment of freedom. In fact, if you want to develop big risk takers then celebrate their failures.

TRAINING PEOPLE TO HEAR GOD

The first time you lead ministry time you will probably have to teach your group how to hear God's voice. You are probably going to have to continue this teaching for the first few weeks until people catch on, and every time a new person comes. If people know the win, but can't hear God, nothing much is going to happen.

Hearing God

All believers can hear God (John 10:3-6). He speaks to us all the time. People who are not accustomed to hearing God think that silence is normal. God sees the issue differently. He is talking all the time, but people don't recognize His voice.

For God does speak—now one way, now another—

though man may not perceive it.

In a dream, in a vision of the night,

when deep sleep falls on men

as they slumber in their beds (Job 33:14-15).

Teach Me Please

The number one reason people do not hear God's voice is because no one has taught them how. Many are thinking, "If God wanted to speak to me, then I would hear an audible voice. "

God's first language isn't English. He is Spirit and communicates things to our spirit. If someone doesn't know how to recognize how He speaks, then they are going to miss what He's saying.

Before your first ministry time with a small group, it is best to take 20-25 minutes and teach the different ways God supernaturally speaks. If you don't have time, skip to the words of knowledge section.

I used to teach how to hear God's voice by sharing a list of the ways that God speaks, as well as telling testimonies from my experiences and my friends' experiences of hearing God. This was my list:

- Nature (Romans 1:20, Psalms 19:1-3)
- The Spirit's conviction (John 16:8)
- Prophecy (1 Peter 4:11,1st Cor.14:24-25)
- Dreams (Job 33:14-18)

- Signs and wonders (Matthew 27:50-54),

- Trances or Visions (Acts 10:10-13),

- A Voice Audible Only to Your Ears (1 Samuel 3),

- Audible Voice (Acts 9:3-4, John 12:28-29),

- Angels (Luke 1:26-27),

- A personal visitation (Numbers 12:6-8, John 14:9).

I have found that some people got excited, but often concluded that I was some type of Christian Superstar, which meant they could never be like me. Others thought I was really, really crazy.

So I changed my teaching method, which increased my ability to help the people I was ministering to. Now I just read off a few items at a time, and verses. I then ask, "Has anyone ever had God speak to them in this way?" The responses are astounding. Atheists will share about the time they thought they saw an angel. Cessationists will share about the time God spoke to them audibly while they were praying. It turns out that most people have had supernatural experiences, they have just forgotten about them. When you ask people to share their stories it jogs their memory, and they often respond, "Maybe I do believe in this stuff?"

When you have the people in your group share their stories of hearing God, some cool dynamics take place. It makes the supernatural believable. Some will think, I may not have a lot of experiences, but Tim has a really cool story. He seems to have a lot of integrity so I can believe him. Maybe this stuff is for real.

Secondly, it normalizes the supernatural. "Hey, this stuff is happening to a lot of people that are just like me. I guess it could happen here."

It is normal for your group not to have God speak to them in every way mentioned on the list. Before I teach on this subject I always make a list of testimonies for each item so I will have something to share if needed.

After we get done, I teach the group how to recognize words of knowledge. Most of the time God will communicate to your group members through words of knowledge. These are not lesser forms of communication. God speaks this way frequently probably because it is the way He likes to do things. The following are examples of words of knowledge:

Pictures: Close your eyes, and imagine that you see an apple. The place where you see the apple is the movie screen of your mind. Often pictures will show up on this movie screen. Sometime they will be still shots, and other times they will be like videos.

Pain: You may experience pain in an area of your body that you don't normally have pain. This is often a sign that God wants to heal someone with that pain.

Highlights: Sometimes a person will stand out to you, or a part of their body will be highlighted to you.

Senses: You may smell something, taste something, hear something, feel something, see something, or experience something emotionally.

Phrases: Sometimes you will hear a word or part of a sentence or a complete sentence.

Knowing: Sometimes you will just know that X is what God is doing, or what He wants you to pray or say.

Unstopping the Well

The Holy Spirit is supposed to be a stream of living water bubbling up inside of us. Some people have a hard time connecting with Him. For some, it is because they have been taught to suppress parts of their personality. When you grow up in an environment where you are taught to suppress pieces of yourself unknowingly, the Holy Spirit can be treated like one of those parts.

Unlearning suppression is very difficult. I tell people who have this difficulty to spend time daily placing their hands on their heart, and focus on the idea that God's love is radiating toward them. We are spiritual beings. Our spirit is the part of us that connects to the supernatural realm. When we focus our thoughts on God our spirits begin to recognize Him.

If during this time sin comes to mind, we need to confess it. If we have sinned against someone, settle in your heart to go and apologize to make things right. However, anything beyond that is not from the Lord. You need to intentionally stop focusing on guilt and return your thoughts to God. "Godly sorrow brings repentance that leads to salvation and leaves no regret, but worldly sorrow brings death (2 Cor. 7:10)." There is a type of sorrow for sin that kills our relationship with God, and it comes from the accuser of the brethren. We must avoid it at all costs. Once sin is confessed it is done. We are sinning by not letting it go. What God says about us is more true than how we feel. He says our sins are forgiven, and we have to place our faith in His word.

Baby Steps

For those to whom it is completely new to listen to the Spirit, dialing down and waiting on God will be a little too much at first. So take baby steps. People grow the fastest through baby steps as they are small steps outside of someone's comfort zone. They are small enough not to be overwhelming. When ministry is overwhelming it causes people to shut down and quit. When people don't go outside of their comfort zone they atrophy. In fact, every time your group is learning a new ministry skill it is best to take baby steps. The following exercises are great to do with a new group:

1. Ask the Lord to bring to mind a Bible verse to share with the group. Encourage them to dial down and listen for about a minute. Then have people share the verse, and how God brought it to mind. Did they see it, did they think about it, or did God remind them of a Bible story? This does two things,

it gets people more comfortable stepping out, and the Bible is safe. You can't "miss it" with a Bible verse.

2. Pick a person. Tell the group something like, "What we are going to do is share words of encouragement with (Person's name). I want you to dial down. We are going to ask the Lord to bring to mind ways this person has encouraged us, and to listen to see if God has anything He wants to say." This does several things at once. The first is that your group is learning to encourage. If you can't encourage people, then you will not be good at prophesying. Prophecy is meant to build up the body (1 Cor. 14:3). Secondly, encouragement often releases prophetic words. When I am ministering in public, and I don't have any prophetic words, I will focus on something that I like about the person, and share it with them. As I do, I often get a download of the prophetic. Many group members will experience that. Thirdly, your group is listening to God without pressure to hear.

3. Pick a person in the group, and say, "Let's ask Jesus what He likes about (Person's name)." Ask the group, "If Jesus were to walk in the room, what do you think He would say to Jim?" This is a little more advanced. We are listening this time for what God thinks, but if someone is a little off it is usually still positive.

4. Conclude the group by saying, "Let's take a few moments and listen to God to see if He wants to take things in a different direction. If you feel like you are getting a word, or feel led to

pray, feel free to step out." If no one gets anything after three or four minutes, then end the ministry time, and debrief.

You may have to repeat these exercises for the first couple of meetings until the group starts to become competent doing them.

Helping the Analytical

Analytical people often complain that they have a difficult time hearing God because they are so logical and rational. Actually, some of the most anointed prophetic people that I know are very analytical.

One way to help analytical people hear God is by teaching them the difference between hearing God as a mathematician, and hearing God as a scientist. Mathematicians plug data into formulas in order to get the correct answers. However, God doesn't give us a formula for hearing Him.

Scientists, on the other hand, are analytical people who use a different method for reaching conclusions. First they encounter a phenomenon. Then they form a hypothesis about what is going on. Then they test it out to confirm or deny their hypothesis.

When you approach God like a scientist you look for any phenomena that might be God's voice, such as a random thought or picture that pops into our mind. Then you form a hypothesis "This may be God speaking" or "This may not be God speaking." Then you test it out by sharing it with the group. "I think this may be God saying X." Then you need to get feedback from the group or person you are praying for in order to confirm or deny it. If it is God, then you have discovered a new fact. If it is not God, then you have discovered a new fact as well.

Collaboration

One major hindrance for those who are new to hearing God's voice is the expectation that they have to go through this process alone. It is normal when a person receives a word of knowledge for them not to know who it is for, what it means, or if it is something that they have made up or if it's from God. Prophets experience this all the time.

It doesn't mean that the person is doing something wrong. It means they are doing something right. God intentionally gives the word in that format so that the receiver will share it just as it is. Many people don't realize this and they keep waiting for more. Or they don't share because they are afraid of looking stupid or missing it. A good coach helps reduce that fear by making sharing socially acceptable. If they don't share in that moment, they will miss what God may be doing.

In most parts of the world school teachers are mandatory reporters. A mandatory reporter is someone whose job it is to share any suspected child abuse or neglect with a state agency. It is not the teacher's job to discern and prove that abuse is going on. Their job is to simply share whenever they have a suspicion that abuse might be taking place. The members of your small group are mandatory reporters of God's voice.

When people are learning, I tell them that they have one job and that's to be a mandatory reporter in sharing what they experience. It's not to decide if what they have is the interpretation or the application. The group will help them decide those things. Their job is to simply report what they are experiencing. You can't be right or wrong about reporting your experiences.

Helping the Burnt

Burnt people have had really bad experiences due to improperly trained prayer ministers. They fear getting hurt again, and want to avoid it at any cost. However, there is a big difference between avoiding unhealthiness and pursuing health. One is running away from something, and the other is running toward something. Most burnt people don't discern the difference. So they will have difficulty feeling safe during ministry time no matter how healthy it is.

One way to help burnt people is to acknowledge that their experience is real, and you will create a safe environment. Then help them recognize that some people have positive experiences during ministry time, and that you want to promote that. I have found it effective to challenge burnt people to stop running, and start being the solution by modeling for others how to minister in a healthy way. I tell them the only way for things to change is by them showing the world it can be done differently.

Helping the Skeptical

Skeptics need information. They need time just to sit and watch. Give them both. Once they start to have a few positive experiences many will be hooked, and start praying for others.

Dealing with Fears

There are two major fears that constantly surface when leaders teach about the supernatural. The following ways have been very effective for me in eliminating these fears:

Fear 1: My Small Group Leader is Crazy and Making Things Up

No one wants to be tricked. We are afraid of con artists and rightfully so. People who believe in the supernatural seem crazy to the rest of the world. Some actually do have mental issues.

The only thing you have to set yourself apart is your integrity. If you want people to set aside their fears and follow you in the pursuit of the supernatural, then you have to preserve your integrity at all costs. Never fluff up a story in order to make it sound better than it really is. The rule I live by is "Undersell and over deliver." When I tell testimonies I talk about my fears, and how I checked things out to make sure it was in fact God. People with integrity check things out. If you start to share your healthy skeptical side, it will add an extra layer of validity to your testimonies.

Fear 2: What if this leads to Heresy?

Heresy is a legitimate fear. We don't want to do things that are against Scripture. That is why we need to teach people how much we value Scripture. When I teach on hearing God's voice I emphasize my value for Scripture.

God speaks most clearly and accurately through the Scriptures (2 Peter 1:20-21, 2 Timothy 3:16-17). It is a common trend to neglect the Scriptures for more "supernatural" means of communication. This is dangerous because the Scriptures teach us the difference between truth and error.

The Scriptures are the standard against which we measure any form of communication from God that we receive. Prophecies, doctrines or ideas that contradict the Scriptures are not communication from God (I John 6:3-4a). An anti-theologically based approach to hearing from God is a breeding ground for heresy (2 Timothy 4:3). That's why I tell people that we should judge everything, hold on to the good and reject the bad (1 Thes 5:19-22). As John Wimber used to say, "Eat the meat and spit out the bones."

CELEBRATING DIFFERENCES

Most people go through similar life stages. When babies are born, they sleep most of the day, and need lots of attention. Eventually, the baby will learn to eat, and talk. Before you know it there is the first day of school, then there is middle school, then high school. After that there is marriage, having children, and then retirement.

Part of being a parent is walking your child through those stages. As your child grows, you change the way you relate to them. You parent a child differently at age 2 than age 40.

Since almost everyone has the same stages to process, you can learn how to navigate these stages through reading books and articles for helpful tips. However, as any experienced parent will tell you, a book can't teach you everything you need to know about how to parent because every child is different. So one's parenting techniques must be individualized for the child.

The same is true for coaching prayer ministers. Everyone goes through a similar path in development, but each one is unique. You must learn to coach in a way that helps them develop through each stage, individualizing things to meet each person's unique needs and journey.

You Have to Get This

Everyone is different. You are probably aware of this, but do you believe it in the core of your being? God made people unique intentionally. He treats people differently. Jesus spent more time with the Jews than the Gentiles, more time with the disciples than the Pharisees, and more time with Peter than Judas. Treating every person differently was a part of Jesus' strategy for reaching the world. Our culture says that everyone should be treated the same, thus we get hooked on formulas as the answer. You have to meet each person where they are at, in order to help that person grow from where they are presently. Which simply means you must treat each one differently.

There is something in our culture that says we need to be fair but if we look at scripture, fair is not a biblical term. It doesn't say, "be fair one to another, " but rather teaches us to do the right thing in love which can look like correction, grace or something else entirely. The point is that we must coach people differently based on where they are at. You will have to adjust how you coach to where they are in the learning process, and how God has made the person, and gifted them. Below are some different categories of people you will encounter as you lead.

Beginners

Beginners have little-to-no clue what they are doing. They need for you to direct them. Most want an expert (you) to tell them exactly what to do, step-by-step, and how to do it. Remember, there will always be those who don't want direction, but they still need it.

Offer to lend them books, DVDs, CDs, and MP3s. I often ask people, "Would you like to read this, and tell me what you think?" This sets us up for a conversation where I can answer their questions. Every church that wants to grow mature, Spirit-led disciples has to have a method for getting information to enthusiastic beginners.

When doing ministry time, spot coach these people more than others. Teach them in one to two minutes how to hear from God, or pray for the sick before and during ministry time. People will pretend like they don't need it to hide their lack of training, but internally they will be grateful and will feel more included. Try to direct something like this to the whole group so that the beginner does not feel singled out.

The Disillusioned

The disillusioned are people who have had access to the right information, but have not seen a lot of fruit, and are not sure that it will work for them. Learning to walk in the Spirit is a huge learning curve. However, some churches act like that isn't the case. They send people to attend a seminar, or a small group, and then they move on to the next topic.

The people you serve need you to ask good questions to draw out answers that will reveal what is really causing them to be stuck. Intentionally ask them where they feel they are growing or where they would like some help. Let them know about your own struggles that you faced as you grew and how you overcame them.

The Discouraged

The discouraged have some testimonies under their belts, but they have bloodied their nose a few times. They don't need more information; they just need encouragement and support. The word encourage means to give someone courage; it's about changing people's focus from where they feel disappointed to where they have seen God move. I have learned do this by retelling people about their success and the growth that I have seen them make, as well as reminding them of God's greatness. Encouragement has to become a spiritual discipline if you want to maintain a kingdom culture.

The Skeptical

Skeptics come at all levels, some are open but need convincing, while others are adamantly closed and opposed to the supernatural. All need direction, respect, and love. You can help the open skeptic by giving them time. Most just want to watch and check things out to see if you are the real deal.

The Burnt

Someone who is burnt has most likely gone through bad experiences in churches. They have been damaged by what others have said and done; hype has turned them off. Now is the time for them to heal and deal with any lies they learned during those times.

A major lie is that time heals. Time does not heal, but truth does. The truth is that a burnt individual has had a bad experience by misguided church ministers. The truth also is that God does supernatural things today, and He calls every member of His church to participate.

Burnt people want to run away from environments where they were burnt, such as ministry time. There is a big difference between running away and running toward something. Start by helping them to identify what they are running from. I ask them questions to get to the root of the issue.

"What caused this? Was it unhealthy prophetic words, bad doctrine, hype, authoritarianism, spiritual abuse, religiousness, etc? Let's first identify what happened."

Until they can name the real issue, they can't distinguish healthiness from unhealthiness. We trying to help them prevent throwing the baby out with the bath water.

Secondly, they have to develop a vision for healthiness. Challenge their perspective by asking them: "I know what you are against, but what are you for? Are you for healthy and powerful ministry time? What if it is possible? Are you willing to be a model for others of how to pray in a healthy way?"

When people experience burns in real life, a doctor will continue to pull skin and tissue off the person for weeks to keep them from getting infected and to promote healing. They will also pull scar tissue off which is very painful. This same process has to happen for a spiritually burnt person if they want to find healing. They must intentionally go into environments that are out of their comfort zone, and experience the pain of being in situations that they cannot control.

The Mature

The mature are people who get it. They are relationally healthy, and when they pray, people consistently experience God. These people need two things from you: bigger challenges, and an opportunity to train others. This will communicate that you trust them. You might start by lending them a copy of this book, and sending them people to coach. Use the "You watch me. We do together. I watch you. You train others." method.

Those More Gifted Than You

You will have people in your group that are more gifted than yourself in some areas. That can be intimidating but remember you are there as an equal to come alongside them in whatever way you can. The problem is that when you cannot speak into someone's life, you have an unhealthy bond with that person. Christians are organs in the body of Christ. We have to give and receive from other organs to grow. Your positional authority gives you permission and obligation to give feedback to anyone under your care.

I have a friend named Wayne who is extremely prophetic and this used to intimidate me. I knew I had positional authority over Wayne as his small group leader, but I knew he had a level of spiritual authority that I didn't have.

I asked him to have breakfast with me to talk about this. However, before I could say a word, Wayne told me, "A lot of pastors don't have the courage to pursue the supernatural. I am proud of you." Wayne didn't see me as someone who didn't know what he was doing. Although I didn't know what I was doing, he was rooting for me. People who love God love to see less experienced people grow because the closer you get to God, the more you want to see God's love spread.

You need not feel intimidated, or suppress someone who is more gifted than you in a particular area. Make room for them to shine. I have seen leaders lose very mature people because they feared losing status. If someone is more gifted, have fun learning from them and ask them to mentor you as you lead.

GIVING FEEDBACK

Everyone has blind spots. People can be blind to their weaknesses as well as their strengths. Feedback shines a light on the areas we cannot see. This is why giving feedback is a coach's primary job. A coach is to be the iron that sharpens iron. If you are waiting for someone to ask what you think, then you aren't doing your job well. How you give it will either cause people to thrive or harm them long term. Therefore, it's essential that you learn how to give feedback and make yourself do it until you feel comfortable with it.

Catch Them Doing it Right

Rewarding someone for doing something right is one of the most powerful and underused teaching tools in the universe. I was impacted by this significantly in college. I was given the assignment to train a rat to push a bar 30 times consecutively. The rat was placed in a box with transparent walls. On one wall was a bar, at the rat's foot was a tray, and I would push a button that would release a pellet of food into the tray. The food was meant to be a reward for good behavior. Every time the rat did something right I would reward it with food. At first, I would give it food simply for looking at the bar. However, the rat didn't understand what it did to receive the food but since I was not feeding it very much, it was very motivated to find out. Eventually it caught on, and started looking at the bar regularly. After that, I raised the stakes a little, only giving food when it reached toward the bar. At first the rat was confused. The reward had stopped coming, and it didn't know why. For a while it would look at the bar and nothing would happen. Then once it accidentally raised its paw toward the bar, and suddenly food fell. A long time passed again. It would look up, and seem frustrated. Then from just crawling around in the box its paw would happen to go near the bar, and again, more food. The pattern repeated itself again and again. Once it learned to meet my requirements, I would raise the standard on what I would reward. After it mastered reaching for the bar, I would raise the standard to touching the bar, then pushing the bar down once. Then twice, then five, 10, 20, 25 times. After several months, eventually it got to 30 times consecutively. I took away from this experiment a profound lesson. I had trained the rat entirely through positive reinforcement, never punishing it.

If you praise your prayer ministers when you notice forms of incremental improvement, they will improve dramatically over time. Don't just tell them they've done a good job, be specific so that they know what they've done right. Say something like, "I noticed that you stepped out, and your prophetic word was dead on. I love your boldness." As they grow, increase what it takes to receive praise.

Secondly, you can increase the rate at which they learn by asking good questions. When a person does something right, ask them, "Why did you do it that way?" Also, help them to connect their behavior with positive feelings. Positive feelings are rewards in themselves, and will increase the behavior in the future. God wants us to enjoy serving him. Even when times are hard, He wants us to look forward to joy. Jesus is the best example of this. It was for the joy set before Him that Christ endured the cross (Heb. 12:2).

Most coaches have a disposition to spot what is wrong in others and in themselves. Also, most prayer ministers feel like failures when they first start out because they are not seeing a lot of fruit. If you only give feedback when a person is doing something wrong, they will get discouraged, and start to avoid you. If you have ever had a boss who was never pleased with you, you know what this feels like.

Try an experiment. Make it a goal to praise people for doing the right thing and don't use negative feedback for a week. So if 9 out of 10 people show up to small group late, don't complain, you can simply say, "I want to thank everyone who showed up on time. It means a lot, I know you rushed to get here." What if you praised the people at work who were doing their jobs right instead of pointing out what they are doing wrong? What would it do for those people? What if you told those who stepped out for the first time that you were proud of them? What do you think would happen? How would those people feel? How would you feel?

Out of the last ten times that you have given feedback what percentage has been positive or negative? Do people look forward to hearing from you? When was the last time that you praised someone for what they were doing right? Who could you do that for right now?

One-on-One

The fastest way to see people grow is through one on one mentoring. These are times to answer people's questions, encourage them, and give some helpful corrective direction. Typically, I try to do to this with a person after everyone leaves group or over coffee. If you only do one-on-one time when things go wrong, people will come to dread their time with you. But when you meet with them every few weeks, you will become more of a mentor.

Small group coaches perform the function of a pastor, caring for and feeding the sheep. Pastoring differs from teaching. Teaching primarily develops people with information whereas pastoring primarily develops people through relationships. Relationships are messy and painful; sheep bite sometimes, and it hurts. If you want to be a teacher, lead a Sunday school class not a small group. Shepherds have to clean up a lot of sheep poop. If you want to coach, you will be involved in several challenging one-on-one conversations. These conversations will be very painful at times, but will shape people for years to come.

Addressing Edges

Everyone has an edge, especially new prayer ministers. Edges are the broken parts of us that hinder the Spirit or harms those to whom we minister. Sometimes it is a bad attitude or the fear of man, other times it is over exaggeration or fear of intimacy. What keeps most people from ministering effectively is one or two edges.

Addressing edges is the part of the job I struggle with the most. I used to rationalize not having these conversations under the guise of not wanting to hurt someone's feelings, but then I realized that lots of people in the group were feeling hurt by another person's edge. I also realized I was not concerned about their feelings as much as avoiding the pain of having the talk. Deep down, I didn't want my feelings hurt should the person reject me or critique me. I learned that I was robbing a person from the gift of feedback.

Seek First to Understand

We assume we know why a person acts they way do, but those assumptions are often wrong. The best way to find out what's really going on is to simply ask for clarification. Try using the phrase, "Could you help me understand..?"

"Could you help me understand why you told Timmy that his grandmother died because of a lack of faith?"

"Could you help me understand why you're late for the last four meetings? What's going on?"

You don't understand someone until you grasp exactly what they are trying to communicate, and you can tell the person what they are thinking, and they agree that you are accurate.

Often times as someone shares why they did what they did, they will correct themselves or ask you what they need to do.

Use Questions Instead of Advice

Questions draw things out of people; advice puts them on the offensive. I could encourage someone to stop using unhealthy theology or I could ask them to stop using it. I could tell someone to show up on time or I could ask. Which sounds better: "Stop being late," or, "Would it be possible to be here at exactly 7PM from now on?"

When you ask someone something, you are giving them choices in freedom to make their own decision. As a result, when they say yes, they are more than likely to do it because their integrity will be on the line.

Speaking the Truth In Love

If we want to have a kingdom culture, we must learn to navigate relationships by using a communication style that honors God, others, and ourselves. The Bible calls this "speaking the truth in love" (Eph. 4:15). Speaking the truth can be anything from saying what the

Bible says on a topic to accurately defining reality. It can also mean stating what you truly think or feel accurately. We also know that "love always protects" (1 Cor. 13:7) which means that we protect others as much as possible with the words we choose.

Loving people doesn't mean that you can protect them from all pain. Loving simply means saying necessary things in the kindest way possible. Sometimes the truth hurts no matter how kindly it is put. Sometimes we have to hurt others for the sake of the relationship, as is said in the book of proverbs: "Faithful are the wounds of a friend" (Proverbs 27:6).

Most people are so afraid of hurting others that they don't say what needs to be said, and they end up harming the relationship. Henry Cloud, author of *Necessary Endings*, defines hurt as a temporary pain that we cause in another with the intention of good, while harm is when we permanently damage a person or relationship. We have to learn to hurt people in order to protect from harm. Imagine a child has diabetes. The child will die without an insulin shot. If the parents love their child, they will hurt the child and give the shot. It would be selfish for them not to give the shot because they didn't want the child to be mad at them for administering it.

The people in your group need corrective direction just like that diabetic child needs an insulin shot. If they don't get it, they will only damage themselves as well as others, causing them to plateau at the level they currently minister. A loving coach hurts people all the time but seldom harms them. An unloving coach harms people all the time and seldom hurts them. A loving coach hurts those who harm others. An unloving coach allows others to harm people and says nothing out of fear of being misunderstood.

Minimal Invasion

When you have to say something hurtful, a loving person uses the most minimally invasive way possible to get the job done. When a person has arrhythmic heart, it often requires the doctor to cauterize a nerve in the heart. There are two ways to do this: you could crack open the chest, take the heart out, and burn the nerve, or you could make a small incision in the leg, send a scope into the heart and cauterize it. Both get the job done. However, it's a lot easier to recover after the second method. If you have to hurt someone, do it as gently as possible. The Bible says, "A man of knowledge uses words with restraint" (Proverbs 17:17).

When I need to have hard conversations, I will sometimes run through what I need to say with another leader, my wife, or write it out. Speaking the truth in love can require preparation so that we can carefully craft our words and, more importantly, eliminate harmful ones. I love this quote by Dorothy Nevill: "The real art of conversation is not only to say the right thing at the right time, but also to leave unsaid the wrong thing at the tempting moment."

When Coaching is Not Fun

No one wants to confront, and when you do, people will sometimes lash back. In order to coach well, you must let God work deep in you. I did not realize the level of man pleasing in my life until I began coaching. At one point in my life, I avoided giving feedback to a unhealthy prayer minister for nearly a year. My team would complain, but I told them they needed to give her time, but in reality, I was afraid of being hurt by her. She harmed a lot of people, and they left the group. When I finally said something she was hurt because I pretended everything was alright for over a year. I would repeat this cycle several times with others before learning my lesson. Looking back on it, I wish I had been willing to face the pain of being honest.

You will have to make many tough calls, and some people are not going to like what happens. God wants to use this to refine your character so that you can learn to give your anxiety to Him, to honor those who disagree with you, and to communicate the truth in love. Peter, the apostle who died upside down on a cross, reminds us, "However, if you suffer as a Christian, do not be ashamed, but praise God that you bear that name" (1 Peter 4:16).

Church Leader

Tips

BUILDING A PRAYER TEAM

Being on a church service ministry team is very different from praying in a small group. When people in your congregation ask for prayer, it will be one of their most intimate encounters at the church. Only place someone on the team after they have completed their learning curve.

John Wimber used to say, "Everyone gets to play." However, we must understand that not everyone gets to play in the same league. It is irresponsible to have children playing football on the same team as pro-athletes. Your team will perform poorly and people might get harmed. If you place people on the prayer line who are not ready, you are setting them up to fail. It's very possible the people who come for prayer will be harmed as a result.

How do you get people ready?

If you want great prayer ministers, you have to train them. So when is a person trained? Is it when they have heard a teacher teach on a topic? Are they trained when they can repeat back what a teacher says? Or are they trained when they live out what a teacher has taught?

Don't assume that a person is trained after they have attended a class. In Hebraic culture, a person was considered trained when their lifestyle changed. For instance, someone was not called a carpenter until they could build a chair. A healthy prayer minister has to be birthed through training. It takes time.

Starting a Prayer Ministry

The best way to build a prayer ministry is to gather the hungry, mature, gifted, and risk takers into a small group to teach them how to follow the Spirit in prayer.

Make the small group a boot camp for getting them in shape. Week after week do the same thing over and over. Teach, pray, and give feedback. Teach, pray, and give feedback. Teach, pray, and give feedback. You will begin to see healthy prayer ministers develop and emerge. When a person is ready, meet with them one-on-one to ask them to be a part of the team.

If you are a senior pastor of a church plant, you are going to have to develop this team. Consider the following before you begin: You have a limited amount of time, energy, and human capital. You don't want to stretch yourself or your congregation too thin. You are going to have to build a children's ministry, a hospitality team, a leadership team, an outreach team, and a worship team. Don't try to birth this until you are certain that you can spend 6 months to a year in the same small group. Secondly, make sure that the people you invite will not strain your other building blocks. Either sit on this for a season, or sit on other building blocks, but remember that you cannot successfully build them all at once.

Criterions for a Prayer Minister

The following are my criteria I use to select my Prayer Team:

- They pray with the Spirit not at Him.
- They minister out of love and compassion.
- They understand kingdom theology and its application to healing, inner healing, deliverance, and prophecy, using it when they minister.
- They have seen supernatural fruit from their ministry.
- A church leader has prayed with this person on multiple occasions and has a good feel for their style.
- They have strong communication/relational skills.
- They have common sense.
- They have character and do what they say they are going to do.
- They are correctable and teachable.

I evaluate people on a case-by-case basis, and always pray about it. When people ask me how to get on the prayer team, I invite them to a small group. I say something like, "I pick my prayer team members from my small group. Come to my small group, and let's pray together and get to know each other without an agenda. If and when I feel like someone is a match, I will approach them." This helps to weed out the uncommitted, and makes no promises to the person who comes.

Be aware when someone wants to be on the prayer team but doesn't want to be a part of a prayer based small group. Often small churches are not selective enough. It is better to have two solid prayer ministers than six mediocre ones who harm people. People desiring prayer can and will wait for someone capable to come to them.

The Prayer Team Leader

On the television show, *The Office*, it was fairly obvious that Michael Scott was a terrible sales manager. How did he get his job? He was a great salesman and then someone promoted him. The Peter Principle is a management principle stating that people are often selected for new jobs based on their past performance. This sets organizations up to fail. A person should be selected on whether or not they have the skills needed for the job. The skill set needed to be a good manager are totally different from the ones needed to be a good salesman. Not only do companies make this mistake all the time, the church also does in the area of assigning prayer team leaders.

Our tendency is to promote the most gifted person to the top. Someone may be really prophetic and have powerful encounters with God, but that doesn't mean that they can lead a prayer team. Consider the prayer team leader a management position. This person needs to be able to:

- Coordinate schedules
- Teach kingdom theology with accuracy and clarity
- Train and develop others
- Pastor people and give feedback
- Clean up relational messes well
- Follow the Spirit and have a track record of fruit

Prayer team leaders do prayer ministry less and less as their team grows. If you love ministering, you might not want this position. Secondly, cleaning up messes is a big part of what you do. If you can't handle conflict on an ongoing basis, the prayer team leader position may not be your calling.

Training Larger Teams

As the size of your church grows, so will the amount of people seeking to be prayer ministers. Eventually, they will not be able to fit inside of a single home, so you will have to expand the amount of home groups or move the training into a classroom. However, you will want to be able to increase the amount of people being trained, without losing the personal coaching dynamic.

This can be done by identifying coaches, and training them. If your church chooses to use the home group model for training prayer ministers, then the new coaches will become home group leaders. If your church chooses to move the training into a classroom, then the session will look like a teacher teaching, and then having breakout 30 minute sessions. During this time 8-10 potential prayer ministers can be under the care of a coach.

LARGE GROUPS

Leading in a large group is similar to leading a small group except the stakes are higher because any mistakes have a greater impact. You still have to listen to God and take risks, but of course as the size of the group grows, so will the diversity of the population. Not only will you have the hungry, the risk-takers, and the mature in the room, but you will also have the apathetic, cynical, skeptical, the burnt, as well as some unbelievers.

This is why I recommend using baby steps if you are transitioning a church service from one that doesn't have ministry time to one that does. There are several ways to structure ministry time in large groups.

Minister to Congregation

The pastor can minister to the congregation on their own. I have learned to do this if the Lord prompts, but ministering solo stretches me. For starters, I am brain dead after delivering a message which makes focusing really difficult. Secondly, I value teams, and I want to use other people and let our gifts work together.

Using the Prayer Team

There are various ways you can use a prayer team to facilitate ministry time. The simplest way is to invite the team to come up front after the service, then direct the congregation to come forward for prayer.

The pastor needs to have a cue to signal the prayer team members to come forward. Some pastors call for them at the end of the service, while others tell their teams to meet up front at the close of the service.

Inviting The Congregation Forward for Prayer

The people in your church need prayer. Some have illnesses; others have dying parents. Some have teenagers that are out of control. If you end your service saying, "If you would like prayer, come forward," then what people may hear is, "If you need prayer about the sermon topic, come forward." They might think, "What was the sermon about? Oh yeah, money. I don't need prayer for that."

As the leader, your job is to help encourage people to get prayer when you invite them. Try expanding the invitation for prayer time beyond the topics of your sermon. Also, sharing a relevant testimony or two may motivate people.

I might say something like, "If God is doing something in your heart, I invite you to respond to the Holy Spirit by getting prayer. God really uses prayer to change lives. Last week we had a lady's hip realign. She couldn't walk on it for 5 years but now she can run. Also we had a man who suffered from chronic depression for 15 years set free. If you need prayer for anything, we'd love to pray for you. If you are debating whether or not you should come forward. I understand. You might be tired and want to go home or you are not sure if it is important enough. I can tell you that many times when I made the choice to get prayer I didn't feel like it God touched me. I also want you to know that the prayer ministers will keep your requests confidential. Thank you, we'll see you next week."

I know that seems like a lot to say, but that would take you less than 30 seconds. If you will take the time to say something similar, it will dramatically increase the number of people getting prayer, and thus your church will begin to experience more of the supernatural.

Working with a Prayer Team Leader as a Speaker

I love working with a prayer team leader. It takes the pressure off. By the end of a sermon, I find myself worn out and I realize that others can often do a better invitation to prayer than I can at that moment. Secondly, people often get words of knowledge during the service. They can share them with the leader, and the leader can filter them and share them with the congregation.

Using the Prayer Team to Give Words of Knowledge for Healing

Often at healing conferences, the team will pray for words during the service, and afterwards the minister calls the team up asking them to call out any words of knowledge. Just a note about this: words of knowledge need to be kept as short as possible, such as, "I see a man with a tumor behind his right eye." Try to keep it under 45 seconds if you get more details.

I encourage my team to verify the word by asking the congregation for feedback. Ask them to raise their hand if they identify with the word given, allowing the audience to see that God is at work, building faith and expectation. If you are in a large group, it's best to have the team call out all of their words and then pray for the sick after. This will save a lot of time.

There are two ways to pray for the sick at this point. The first is to invite them forward to get prayer from the prayer team. The second is to have the congregation pray, and those who are not healed can be sent to the prayer team afterwards.

Congregational Prayer

When I have people in the congregation pray for each other, I expect four things to happen:

1. God to show up and do really big things.
2. There will be people present who know nothing about prayer.
3. There will be people present who are timid.
4. There will be people who might have a bad experience from a misguided prayer minister.

Don't let the last three deter you from you using this model -- you just need to be prepared to work with these realities. Your job as a coach is to facilitate an environment that maximizes prayer and minimizes bad experiences. This is done by using the tools you've already learned in order to coach people while you lead ministry time.

Perhaps you're leading a group to pray for the sick. You've finished a sermon about abiding in Jesus and ministering out of rest. You continue to guide the congregation by setting them up for success with a simple explanation of what's happening:

"What we are about to do is pray for the sick. If you have never done this before that's okay, we're going to just pray with the Spirit from a place of rest. Remember a lot of people are new at this so be patient with them; God wants to move in this place more than we do so be expectant for things to happen." It may be best to spot coach them about healing or hearing God at this point depending on the amount of time you have, what the Spirit is doing, and the maturity of the congregation.

Allow the audience to pray for about 5-7 minutes. The first couple of minutes will be spent finding out the person's condition. After you have given them time to pray, ask the people who were healed raise their hands. Take a testimony or two, then have the crowd pray for those who were not healed. Give them about 3-4 minutes this time before taking more testimonies. Encourage those who were not healed to get prayer from the prayer team afterwards.

DEVELOPING A KINGDOM CULTURE

Every group has a culture. Baseball fans have a culture. Soldiers have a culture. Bars have a culture. New York definitely has a culture, and so does your church. A culture describes the values that drive the behaviors of a particular group. If you want to see the supernatural in your church, you've got to build a kingdom culture.

A kingdom culture is one where the congregation lives the kingdom lifestyle; they pray for the sick, go out into the streets, live a repentant lifestyle, and spend time with God privately, etc.

The more people you have living that lifestyle, the more supernatural experiences your church will have. If your people aren't ministering, you don't have a kingdom culture. A church does not start with kingdom culture; they grow into it. It will take time, but it doesn't have to take more than a few years.

What I am going to give you are the power tools for cultural change. It is crucial to understand that using these power tools once or twice will be ineffective. You have to build these into your church's culture taking small steps forward until they become habits.

Show People the Vision

When someone tells me something that sounds too good to be true I typically say, "Show me." I want more than their word. Words get people interested but seeing transforms them. If you want people to start praying for the sick on the streets, they have to see the supernatural. Your job is to show them.

People believe what they can see. I didn't believe in miracles until I saw one with my own eyes. The first one I saw was at a conference. During ministry time, the speaker asked who was healed and fifty people raised their hands. I spent the next hour asking people to tell me what happened. I approached them skeptically, asking hard questions, but left convinced.

You may not flow in the supernatural yet, you may have never seen a miracle in your life, but know that this is okay, you can take people to another church where it is happening.

Ask yourself, what church ministry do you want to become more like? Where do you know people who are experiencing God's power in amazing ways? Go and check it out. If it's legitimate, bring your people. If you have to, fly your leaders to where the supernatural is happening. It is money well spent. It's time we make the switch from vision casting to vision showing. Make it a habit that your church community attends these types of events until your church develops a kingdom culture.

On a side note it is a good rule of thumb to avoid taking your people to a conference where you are not familiar with the speakers. Before you attend, listen to some of their material, and read some of their books. In the same way you can't put a bullet back into a gun, you cannot unexpose people to unhealthy ministry experiences.

Bringing in Others

Most pastors recognize that there are areas they are weak in, such as healing, the prophetic or power evangelism, so they avoid teaching on those topics. Others will try to teach from their weaknesses.

If you feel this way, simply understand that you are a part of a body with many parts. So learn to use those other parts. Bring in others to teach. They don't have to be the best in the world, just stronger at it than you are. If you aren't seeing healing, find other churches who are. Invite their staff to your church to teach and train, or have guest teachers speak on Sunday morning. Sunday is prime time for cultural change. Here again we find the "show me" principle.

It not wise to just invite senior leaders. Senior leaders frequently have similar gift mixes, so look for practitioners from other churches who bear lots of fruit. You want to show your people others just like them who are doing ministry effectively, so that they will believe they can do it themselves. Start by bringing in someone every few months. As your church begins to appreciate this, you can do this more frequently.

Teaching On the Supernatural

You get what you teach. Francis McNutt in The Nearly Perfect Crime documents the death of the healing ministry in the church. He says that the church had a vibrant healing ministry for the first 300 years of its existence. After this time, Constantine, the Roman emperor, changed the law so that the church was no longer persecuted. It became fashionable to be a Christian, and many people began entering the church who really weren't concerned about living the kingdom lifestyle. Ministry shifted from the layman to the priest to protect people from heresy; this is when the church stopped teaching the layman how to pray for the sick. The gift of healing began dying out and eventually prayer for the sick became a last rite, with only the priest praying for the sick on their deathbeds. Over time, the church forgot how to pray.

If you want an empowered church, you are going to have to develop a system for training the next generation. Ask yourself this, "How are people that are new to our church supposed to learn about the kingdom, spiritual gifts, hearing God, inner healing, healing, and deliverance?" If you cannot answer that question, then you need to make a place for it, so that you don't quench the Spirit if and when the current leadership or church members move on. The average church member changes churches every five years, which means that the people you train today may not be around tomorrow. Implement things that will equip and encourage both the new and seasoned members.

Tell Testimonies

You get what you celebrate. Weight loss groups have testimony time to motivate others to lose weight, just as recovery groups have people who have recovered tell their story. Salesmen tell "testimonies" at sales meetings to motivate others to sell more.

If you want a church that sees signs and wonders, tell testimonies. Remember what Bill Johnson said, "When people tell testimonies, their faith and expectations increase. When their faith and expectations increase, they are more likely to step out. When they step out, they are more likely to see miracles. When people stop hearing testimonies, they forget how powerful God is, their expectations decrease, and so they stop stepping out. Because they stop stepping out, they stop seeing miracles."

Allow your members to tell their testimonies. When you allow someone to share from the front, they do need some guidelines. You can write them on a 3x5 card and hand it to the person.

- Keep it under 45 seconds. (If you say a minute that can mean anything from 60 seconds to 5 minutes in people's minds).
- Start with the conclusion first. (This will keep people from rambling).
- Make Jesus the Hero so that He gets the glory.

Make Time in Your Schedule

The testimonies that matter the most are the ones that the senior pastor tells. If you are stepping out each week, you will have testimonies. Pastors have to make time to do ministry just like they do for staff meetings and sermon preparation. If you have never learned to lead ministry time, then schedule a time to lead a small group each week. Also, make time to go to the streets. John Wimber used to say, "The meat is in the streets." That's still true.

However, never go to the streets by yourself. I have found that it is really hard to get people to minister one evening each week as well as go to small group. However, about 25 - 35% of your church has free time during the day. Capitalize on that by inviting people out during the day, and if you can find just one person to accompany you, that's enough.

Start small. Hand out popsicles in the park or simple sandwiches at an outdoor event. Keep pushing yourself out of your comfort zone. Eventually, you want to find yourself at the point where you are going into the darkest areas of your city. Jesus always went to the most rejected, ostracized people of the day. They saw the kingdom long before the church people did. God does powerful things in these areas because light shines the brightest in the darkness.

Training People to Recover

When someone falls off a bike, what should they do? Get back on it. When someone strikes out, what should they do? Forget about it, and focus on their next time up to bat. When someone doesn't see the kingdom come, what should they do? They should pray for people again as soon as is reasonable.

When I was first learning to pray for the sick, I prayed for someone and nothing happened. I felt like a failure, and I waited six months before I did it again. People have to be taught how to recover quickly when they aren't successful, or they will not step out frequently.

You will have to train them to give their worries to God, to refocus on His goodness, to take their pain to Him and get back on their bicycle again. The best way to teach this is to model it. We often don't want to appear weak or incapable, but it's important as a leader to allow others to see your imperfections and hear your mental process so that they are encouraged to continue. As you reposition yourself to minister again, others will follow your example in faith and hope.

Pastor People Through the Mess

Developing a kingdom culture can be really messy. People will make a lot of mistakes, and this will cause you and your team an exponential increase in the amount of time you have to spend pastoring. The only way to cultivate a kingdom culture is to pastor it. There is a proverb that is very relevant to this that says,

"Where there are no oxen, the manager is empty, but from the strength of an ox comes an abundant harvest" (Prov. 14:4).

Basically what this proverb says is that it takes something living to produce a harvest. If you want something that is mess free, then you can't have something that is living. If you want something that is living, then you are going to have to deal with a lot of poop in your manger. If you want a kingdom culture, you have to train people to live with a little poop, to clean it up quickly, and help them when they can't do it themselves. If you don't pastor, people will get burnt-out and quit.

Model it

People don't follow ideas, they follow people. You carry the most influence in your organization so in order to see your people change, you have to change yourself. Don't be a consultant, be a practitioner. A consultant is one who reads something in a book, and then tells others to do what they just read. A practitioner is someone who lives a lifestyle and teaches others. The church world is full of consultants but if you want to change a culture, you have to be a practitioner.

Keep Going

The reason most churches don't have kingdom cultures is because they are hard to build. I know how hard it is and that sometimes you want to quit. When I reach a low point, the Lord sometimes reminds me of a story my drill sergeant told our platoon: "Private Cantrell was in the jungles of Vietnam when his platoon was ambushed. He was sitting close to two of his friends. From out of nowhere, the enemy began firing at them. They hit the ground, and began returning fire. The enemy threw a grenade that landed inches between Private Cantrell and his friends. Private Cantrell threw himself on that grenade saving his friends' lives. Then when a second grenade thrown, Private Cantrell stood up with blood gushing from his burning flesh and he threw himself on it. Then he died. Now soldiers, if you throw yourself on a grenade and live through it, the Army will fix you up, ship you home, and someone will pin a metal on your crippled body. The newspapers will call you a hero because that's what you will be. Heroes make sacrifices. But the measure of a man is not whether he throws himself on the first grenade; the measure of a man is whether or not he does it a second time. After it has ripped through your flesh, you will know what its sting is like. That's character. If you should find yourself in that situation, don't die a hero. Die a man of character. Are you a hero or are you a person of character?"

I want to end with this idea. One day you will be old and dying. You might be laying in a bed, staring at the ceiling of a hospital with nothing but time on your hands to think. During that time, you will replay your life. You will replay your first kiss, your marriage, and your children's first steps. Then you will replay your years as a senior pastor. You will ask yourself the question, "Did I lead the church God wanted me to lead or did I quit when things got hard? Did I do the stuff or did I sit in my office?" What story do you want to tell yourself on that day? When you are old and dying you will not be able to change things. You don't get your twenties back or your thirties back. You don't get your forties back but you can change things now. Think about it -- meditate on it until it reawakens the fire that drove you to become a pastor in the first place. Then confirm with your life what you have said with your lips on Sunday mornings.

If you do, you will see the kingdom of God come in power in the land of the living. You will taste the powers of the age to come.

What if you just let everything else go? What would happen if you forgot about trying to make people happy? What if Jesus' opinion was the only one you cared about? If it's hard for you, then it's hard. If people leave, then they leave. If it kills you, then it kills you. But whatever you do, do not stop. Die fighting for a great cause. Die serving the King.

Visit SimplyKingdom.com

ABOUT THE AUTHOR

Elijah Stephens dual majored in philosophy and psychology at Covenant College. In 2005, he married his wonderful wife Alison, and began pastoring in the Vineyard movement. Elijah has a passion for seeing the Kingdom of God come in power and touch every realm of society. He studied three years at BSSM. Currently, he trains and develops church leaders around the world. You can find out more about him at SimplyKingdom.com

Made in the USA
Charleston, SC
12 June 2015